Sensual
Intelligence

THE
LOST
IQ

Reclaim the Wisdom, Power,
and *Joy* of Your Body

SHAWNREY NOTTO

© 2022 Shawnrey Notto

All rights reserved. No part of this publication may be reproduced, distributed, or transmitted in any form or by any means, including photocopying, recording, or other electronic or mechanical methods, without the prior written permission of the publisher, except in the case of brief quotations embodied in reviews and certain other non-commercial uses permitted by copyright law.

Ebook ISBN: 978-1-7376992-0-0
Print ISBN: 978-1-7376992-1-7

What is YOUR
SENSUAL INTELLIGENCE™ TYPE?

Take the quiz to find out!
www.Shawnrey.com/Quiz

To enhance the learning in this book,
take the Sensual Intelligence™ Type Quiz.

You will also get your SQ Type Reading Guide!

The SQ Type Reading Guide tells you the specific
Chapters and exercises that are best suited for
you, so you can make the most of this book!

This Quiz is great to share with your friends and partners.

Find out your Sensual Intelligence™ Type,
and unlock the joyful expression of your body!

*To my Mom, Deirdra and my Nana, Cleo.
Thank you for always believing in me, no matter what.*

From your Shawnshine.

TABLE OF CONTENTS

Listen to Your Body	1
Introduction: The Cave of Wonders	4

PART 1. WHY SENSUAL INTELLIGENCE?

1. Seduce Yourself	9
2. Dazzling Darkness	13
3. A Healing Journey	21
4. Know Your Destination – Defining Sensual IQ	27
5. How Did We Lose It?	35
6. Who Is Smart?	44

PART 2: RECLAIMING YOUR SENSUAL BODY

7. Let's Get Sensual	51
8. The Sensual Intelligence Types	67
9. Coming out of the Dark	81
10. The Journey of the Senses	86
11. Embodiment – Connect with Your Body	105
12. Self-Love – Open Your Heart	119
13. Calm Your Mind	134
14. Community	141
15. Consent and Consensual Community	152

Part 3: Your Sensual Expression Journey

16. The 7Ps of Sensual Expression	163
17. Pleasure – The Journey of Delight and Desire	167
18. Play – The Journey of Curiosity and Exploration	182
19. Passion – The Journey of the Fire of the Heart	193
20. Psyche – The Journey of the Soul and Spirit	205
21. Philosophy – The Journey of Wisdom and Truth	212
22. Power – The Journey of Boundaries and Structure	217
23. Peace – The Journey of Inner Tranquility and Nourishment	230
24. Intimacy, Eros, and Relationships	238
Conclusion	246
Acknowledgements	251
About the Author	253

LISTEN TO YOUR BODY

Sensuality—our intimate connection with this world, ourselves, and one another—is a form of intelligence.

Sensuality is a superpower, a pure life force that comes with great responsibility. It is not just the mechanics of the body; it is the quality of how our bodies are in the world. Sensuality can promote well-being and growth, filling us with purpose, aliveness, and connection—or, if it is unconscious, it can wreak havoc and destruction.

Like all forms of intelligence, we can develop our Sensual Intelligence. But we cannot change what we are not aware of. That is where the Sensual Intelligence Type Quiz comes in. The Quiz is an awareness tool that will give you a starting point to increase your Sensual Intelligence. It will tell you your Sensual Intelligence Type. You can find it and other resources to enhance your experience with this book at www.Shawnrey.com/book-resources.

As we awaken and deepen our SQ, we cultivate more pleasure, vitality, and confidence—revitalizing our relationships, a sense of purpose, and connection with ourselves and others.

I hope that by taking the assessment and reading this book, you will gain

- Clearer decision making
- Heightened ecstasy in your body
- Deeper emotional and physical connection with partners
- Greater empowerment to create what you want, and
- More artful communication with others

It's so easy to get caught up in doing, making, and proving ourselves that we forget that life is about being and feeling, not just getting through it. What if we could be nourished by our efforts, be in alignment with who we are, and live life fully expressed?

To do that, we need to have a healthy, sensual relationship with ourselves.

My invitation to you is the same invitation that I have given to all of my clients and myself: listen to the wisdom, power, and joy of your body, and act from there.

This is the power of Sensual Intelligence. And this book is going to show you how to access it!

What to expect in this book

Welcome to a sensual adventure filled with sensual-erotic poetry to keep your senses titillated and detailed activities you can do right now. Use this book to have an embodied experience, not just read passively.

In Part 1 of our Sensual Intelligence adventure, I will share my intimate story of losing and finding SQ. Then we will define Sensual Intelligence, why it is essential, how we lost it, and what happens when we find it.

Part 2 will have all the tools you need to reclaim your Sensual Intelligence, including being in and loving your body. Oh! You don't want to miss the very delicious and erotic Journey of the Senses. Additionally, there are many fun, guided activities that will help increase your SQ right now!

Finally, in Part 3, we will dive into the origins of the Sensual Intelligence Types and Sensual Intelligence Expressions. You will have all the tools to create deeper intimacy and clear expression with yourself and others.

What to expect from me

I am a cis-gender, heterosexual, black woman whose pronouns are she/her, which influences the lens through which I perceive and understand the world. I absolutely will make mistakes and miss things. If I forget you with my words, I'm so sorry. I have written this book with the best intention and all love, and I know that this book will miss the mark for some people.

If you see anything I left out or have insights that I do not, this is an opportunity to continue the conversation, collaborate, and heal community communication. Help add to this movement by offering your voice and making it properly inclusive.

All of our voices are needed. Thank you ahead of time for being in the spirit of lifting each other to be the best we can be.

Welcome to the Art of Sensual Intelligence.

Introduction

THE CAVE OF WONDERS

Darkness surrounds you. Whispers, drips, rustles, and other mysterious sounds echo off of cold, cavernous walls. You want to leave this place, but you stand frozen, stuck in the small space you know is safe, afraid of what dangers you may encounter if you stray from your location. You want to explore, you want to know what is beyond this place that you inhabit, but you do not see the way.

There! Just ahead, you see a faint glow. It pulses, beckoning you. Slowly, you make your way forward, tumbling and scraping your body. You pick yourself up and dust off the grime, and you feel your heartbeat thudding faster with anticipation as you inch closer. You are so near the light that you can feel its heat, but it is still mostly buried and out of reach. You squat down, laying on your belly, and you reach your hand down, down, down, into the abyss. Then your fingertips brush the hot light, you flinch from the heat, and it slips from your grasp and starts to roll away. In that millisecond of contact, you felt something magnificent, something magical that you know you cannot lose.

Now! You reach out quickly, grab it, ready for its sharp heat, and hold it tightly in your palm.

Your breath comes in gasps. The soft glow grows until it illuminates your hand, then your body. Soon everything around you is glowing, and all at once, your world comes to life!

What you have found is the Lost IQ.

The Lost IQ is a world of wonders and treasure that was always present but was lost and hidden from collective awareness. And now, as you lick your lips in wonder at the tastes in the air, as your eyes dilate and contract at the myriad of sights, as your nostrils flare, as your ears twitch, as your skin prickles, and your heart opens, you realize that you have just discovered a whole new way of being.

Think of this book as that illuminating glow, shining a light on an innate, inner knowing that is inside of you.

Be ready to open yourself to a way of living that you have denied for way too long. Your life and your body are the cave of wonders and discoveries. Allow me to be your guide as we go on this journey as you find, reclaim, and embody the wisdom of Sensual Intelligence, as you demystify the stories that have made the mention of sensuality something to fear.

There will be mountains and valleys, places to climb under and through. There will be riddles that unlock secret doors to your consciousness and detours that will lead you to yet another path.

This journey can be challenging and confronting, but it will be well worth it—because it leads you to your treasure: You.

It is time to claim your full intelligence.

Part 1:
WHY SENSUAL INTELLIGENCE?

The first part of our journey will be about getting to know each other. I am making a bold claim: there is a powerful gift inside you that can profoundly change your life. This gift is called Sensual Intelligence (SQ). But you have never heard of Sensual Intelligence. So what exactly is it? And who am I to make such a claim?

Allow me to use this first part of the book to explain Sensual Intelligence, introduce my story, and remove some misconceptions about the nature of sensuality.

Let's get started.

Chapter 1

SEDUCE YOURSELF

> *I sit in bed, naked. The morning sun softly shines orange on my skin. The tiny hairs on my body glow like gold dust. My nipples are like points of darkness on my canvas of brown and burnished gold. I hold a persimmon in my hand; its translucent skin is barely protecting the sweet juice of the fruit's flesh. It sits like a small heart in my palm—a heart the color of the sunrise. A warm heat mixes with the cool breeze that slides through my window, clinking the strands of the crystal bead curtain. Warm sunrise, warm skin, warm breath against warm-colored fruit. Warm lips and hot tongue. My teeth pierce the skin and sweet persimmon bursts forth onto my lips. I take another bite, slurping the citrine-colored flesh that drips thick and rich like pudding down the side of my pinky. I savor the moment as the sun rises down my throat.*

I wrote this on a Tuesday morning in October 2020, in the middle of the COVID-19 pandemic lockdown. The world was experiencing an unprecedented amount of overwhelm, isolation, uncertainty, and fear. People were pushed to the extremes, exacerbating weaknesses and cracks in the system, making it so easy to break—mind, body, and spirit.

I took this time to deepen into a ritual I created years ago: to slow down, listen, and savor the beauty of the present moment, as shown in my own body.

This is Sensual Intelligence.

Sensual Intelligence, the lost intelligence, is a whole lifestyle, existing well beyond sexuality and the bedroom. It encompasses our inner landscape, how we perceive and are perceived in the world.

SQ is essentially the lost art of connecting to your embodied human experience. It has the intelligence of heart, mind, and body connection that allows you to greet every moment as an opportunity with energy and vitality. It manifests as a feeling of joy and wonder with your own body and environment.

"I feel my body!"

"Oh my god! My skin is so soft!"

"I feel so centered. I've never felt so much in my power before, and just—calm."

These are the voices of those who have been on this journey and have found their Sensual Intelligence. When you discover that lost treasure, a distinct sound emanates from your body.

The moans and groans of freedom and spice make you write poetry and dance your life. It can sound like an exultant 'Aaaahhh!' A guttural 'Ooohhhh!' Or maybe an airy and playful 'Eeeee!' No matter what, everyone's sensual sound is different because everyone's journey is their own. What you discover and recover is for you.

Sensual Intelligence is for everyone, no matter your age, gender, sexual preference, relationship status, or type of career you have. If you have ever wanted to express yourself more, be more authentic and courageous, build intimacy, spice up your sex life, then you have been searching for Sensual Intelligence. If you've ever wondered how to feel comfortable with yourself, how to be in your body, find your voice, and grow into the person you have dreamed of becoming, SQ is what you have been looking for.

I will be sharing stories about myself and past clients. I have changed all the names and details of every story to protect privacy. Some of the stories are a compilation of multiple peoples' stories because there are many overlapping experiences. Though most of these stories come from women, this journey is not only for women. I share our stories because I want you to feel each person's depth, personality, and nuance. Every story passes on unique wisdom.

The Sensual Intelligence journey is both deeply intimate and universal. No matter your gender identity and expression, I hope that you find these stories as touching and useful as I do.

You, right now, are doing a beautiful and incredibly courageous act: choosing yourself, even if it feels scary or intimidating. My hope is that this book will allow you to experience yourself as Jade did when she said, "I can't believe how my body has morphed. I've opened up a whole new level of joyful, safe self-expression for me. I laugh and feel completely safe."

When the world stopped in March of 2020, and everyone was forced to spend more time with themselves, many of us realized that who we thought we were was actually who we were told to be, how we thought we should be. We realized that we had not known our hearts, desires, or authentic selves since childhood.

This strange time revealed a choice that was there all along: the choice to connect deeply with ourselves and our body's wisdom. The alternative was to keep our eyes closed, to keep ourselves in the dark.

Sensual Intelligence is how we conduct our bodies in the world with skill and dexterity. We are sensual beings. We gain information utilizing our senses, and we communicate using our bodies.

This full-embodied expression is a living meditation, a path unique to you. It is your path because it is your special body, your past, your stories, your ancestors, your circumstances, your soul signature that beautifully shapes the world. Life is meant for us all to embrace our different contributions to the rich tapestry of life, weaving together an exquisite pattern.

Being on this journey requires you to choose: claim your connection to your body, joy, and sovereignty; or continue believing the stories and roles assigned to you. I made this choice many years ago when I was just 16 years old. In one of the darkest moments of my life, I chose myself, which led to this journey of finding my lost IQ. As a result, I created a life of pure joy, expression, and depth of being, and I want the same thing for you. So I'll be your guide to reclaiming the parts of you that you may have forgotten.

Let me take you back to where it all started.

Chapter 1 Summary

- Covid-19 lockdown forced us to spend more time with ourselves.
- Many of us realized that we're living who we were taught we should be instead of who we are.
- We can find ourselves by slowing down, being present, and listening to our bodies.
- Sensuality—our intimate connection with this world, ourselves, and one another—is a form of intelligence, Sensual Intelligence.

Chapter 2

DAZZLING DARKNESS

> *A great ring of pure and endless light*
> *Dazzles the darkness in my heart.*
>
> *~Madeleine L'Engle, A Ring of Endless Light*

Home Life

Madeleine L'Engle was one of my favorite authors when I was growing up. I became obsessed with the poetry sprinkled throughout her science-fiction novels. I wrote some of those poems on the bedroom walls with glow-in-the-dark chalk so that each night my younger sister and I slept under glowing stars on the ceiling and poetry all around us. This poem in *A Ring of Endless Light* struck a chord with me that reverberates to this day.

You need to have a North Star during difficult times, something that guides you when it feels like the world is falling apart. The thing is, you don't often get to choose your North Star. Instead, it finds you and secretly lodges itself deep in your heart, emerging when you least expect it. You may not even know it is there, helping you remember that you are sacred, divine, and an expression of love. But it is there, and you are being guided even in the darkest times. If you pause, breathe, and open your inner eye, you will see its glimmer, reminding you. This poem in *A Ring of Endless Light* was one of my North Stars.

People experience me now, and they see all joy, smiles, silliness, and confidence. And yes, that's absolutely the way I am today. I love my body, my life, who I am, and how I am. I get to lead workshops and teach people to discover and reclaim their pleasure and aliveness—but I was not always this way. I used to be lost in my own dark cave.

I grew up in a moderately religious household with busy, working parents. My family (mom, dad, younger brother, sister, and I) moved around the United States and Germany because my parents were in the Army. We ultimately settled in Arkansas when I was 11. I was a world-traveled, young, black girl, going through puberty in a racist, bible-belt state. It was a recipe for some deep shit.

My siblings and I were taught to believe in sex only after marriage, and hugs, kisses, and physical affection were rare. It was more important for us to keep our rooms clean and obey our parents than to share loving touch. Because we were not supposed to question parental authority, my relentless curiosity and questioning were considered "sassy," "lowdown," and disrespectful. I would get punished for disobedience and insolence. I didn't know how to play it cool. I had, and still have, all the subtlety of a jackhammer.

I learned a lot about spankings and corporal punishment: like when to hold my breath and which body parts to clench or relax to lessen the pain. I now understand my parents used pain and punishment to teach order, obedience, and structure. I now know that these practices get passed down through the generational trauma of enslavement. Punitive, authoritarian parenting was a survival technique as much as it was a means to keep household chaos at bay. But I did not know that then.

My young, developing body assumed that the pain and punishment I received meant that I was inherently evil. It was not a priority to teach about having a relationship with bodies (other than to tell us not to get pregnant), nor our emotions (unless we were back-talking or being mean to our siblings). Everything about the body was scary, mysterious, and "nasty." So when I found the sexy magazines where the women had no hair on their genitals, I was morbidly fascinated and very confused. I didn't look like that! My body had hair and made weird smells. Yet these explicit, sexualized photos, with precisely groomed genitals, were some of my first teachings about the body.

When my parents found the adult magazines underneath my pillow, my dad further compounded my confusion by punishing and humiliating me in front of the entire family. I got my bare butt spanked in front of everyone. I felt the hot heat of shame in every aspect of that particular punishment. It was ironic that I was punished for looking at naked, sexualized bodies by having my partially naked body spanked in front of everyone. My punishment was an example to show that anything dealing with sex, pleasure, or the body was bad, a sin, and severely punishable.

But this didn't stop me. I couldn't help it. I found the VHS pornography, which I consumed avidly, furtively. I watched, filled with fear, wonder, guilt, and shame. I cried and raged about this every time I looked at one of those 'sinful' films. One time I took my favorite VHS tape and bashed it with a bat, all the while screaming and crying because I knew, from the bottom of my heart, that I was going to hell for my sins.

Finding Your North Star

When I read the words "dazzles the darkness in my heart," from the poem in A Ring of Endless Light, by Madeleine L'Engle, I felt that my darkness could be beautiful and that maybe, just maybe, my darkness could shamelessly occupy the same space as my light.

The possibility that my heart could have darkness and that the darkness did not have to be inherently wrong was a balm to me! Those simple, compelling words told me that I could be loveable in all my fallacies.

- What is your North Star?
- What is the message it wants you to remember?

School

While all of this drama was happening at home, my school had its issues.

I loved school. In part because I was good at it. I worked hard, followed the rules, and earned the validation I couldn't quite achieve at home because of my "sassy" mouth. However, the Arkansas school system brought its version of invisible, authoritarian control.

When I enrolled in middle school in Arkansas, I proudly handed over my report card to the person at the front office, who then handed it to the principal. They took one look at my straight A's and immediately put me in Special Education (S) and Inclusion (I) classes. Inclusion classes integrate special education and learning disabled students with Regular (R) classes.

I didn't know I was in these kinds of classes. I didn't know my own school had racially profiled me. Neither my parents nor I understood the significance of the "(I)" and "(S)" on my class schedule. What I did understand was that these classes were strange and chaotic.

The kids were loud, and the teachers seemed extra strict. I don't think a day went by without someone being sent to the office, given detention, or suspended. And the students were constantly being told how bad they were.

I just kept my nose down and worked hard because I loved learning (and because I was painfully shy and awkward). I did not know I was in the Inclusion class. I thought this was how people acted in Arkansas since everything else was foreign to me. For example, I had never heard of name-brand clothing; I was called "black" even though my skin was chocolate brown. The kids called sodas "pop" and said the way I talked was "white" and uppity.

After a semester of being quiet, keeping my head down, and feeling massive culture shock, I excelled in my classes. Finally, my teachers convened and placed me in advanced Honors (H) classes instead of Inclusion (I) classes.

It was like night and day! Honors classes were 98 percent white kids and had half the number of students. The honors kids could say and do anything they wanted because they were "gifted." The same teachers that screamed and expelled my former classmates for standing up before asking if they could go to the bathroom allowed the honors kids to talk back and be smart-asses. But the teachers would laugh and tell them how clever they were! This incident was my first transparent look at systemic oppression, and though I didn't have the term for it, I knew this hypocritical double standard was wrong.

When I got to high school, I was chosen to participate in a program for gifted African-American youth to give us the tools we needed to have a competitive edge to succeed and give back to our communities as leaders.

The program was the opportunity of a lifetime for a girl like me! I had one-on-one meetings with the head mentor where we discussed college and career prospects and generally received guidance on achieving success in a world where the representation of "success" didn't have my face or background too often.

The head mentor of the program was a white man in his sixties. He was outspoken and opinionated, with an amazing history in activism, civil rights, and education. He was committed to the program and to us young people and pushed us to be our best. I always felt a combination of intimidation and determination when I attended the meetings.

My meetings with my mentor were great at first. We discussed philosophy, psychology, and economics, but I was more interested in human relationships and using humanity, artistry, and psychology to make the world better. I spoke in earnest about being a holistic person, but my mentor was more interested in economics. He often chided me for my dreams, insisting that I couldn't do anything unless I made money first. Once I made money, he said, I would have the resources for the life I wanted, and I could give back.

One day, something shifted that changed everything. After a riveting conversation, he hugged me on my way out. It was fine, and I even felt special—until the hug lingered. Then he leaned down and kissed my neck and grabbed my butt, pulling me closer to him. I froze in shock. I remember trying to tear away from him. I remember how tall he was and how small I felt. I remember how his body blocked the sunlight coming through the big windows of his office.

Then, he let go and told me goodbye as if nothing had happened. As if this was just another day. As if he had not just launched a 16-year-old, never-been-kissed, awkward black girl across an invisible threshold where innocence, safety, trust, and autonomy were on one side and a terrifying world on the other. I left in a daze. To this day, I can still recall the smell of the air-conditioned hallway. I got in the car and drove back home confused, scared, disgusted, and bewildered.

When he violated me, I saw behind a veil that I didn't realize existed. I saw the shadowland that makes up our world, our deepest and darkest secrets, personal and societal. At 16 years old, I was forced to come face-to-face with the unease and wrongness that I felt inside and had been taught. I saw the broken seams of our system. I didn't understand what I was seeing, but I could not unsee it.

I never told anyone. I didn't know how to tell anyone.

I had never talked about sex or anything like that at home. I was ignorant of a lot of things dealing with my body. For example, I accidentally found out what masturbation was when I saw the word written on an information packet. Once a year, we attended an awkward, abstinence-based, sex-education unit during health class. That year, the girls got a goodie bag filled with tampons, pads, and pantiliners. The outside of this turquoise goodie bag was decorated with questions and answers about puberty. This is how I discovered the word masturbation.

Q: "Can I get pregnant from masturbating?"

A: "No, you cannot get pregnant from masturbating."

Naturally, as the curious child I was, I went to my mom.

Me to my mom: "What's masturbation?"

Mom to me: "Don't you ask me anything like that! That's nasty! If you want to know about that kind of thing, you need to look it up in the encyclopedia or the dictionary!"

I was terrified. I didn't know I was asking something forbidden. So I looked it up and found out why the girl in the pamphlet asked if she could get pregnant from masturbation.

Although I kept going to the meetings with this man, it made me sick. Most of the time, on my way out, his hugs would linger, his hands and mouth would roam, and I felt like I was dying inside. I would alternately cry or be numb, calm, and "collected" on the drive home from those meetings. I kept quiet because I was scared that I would not be successful and would not have any opportunities if I didn't stay on his good side.

I wanted a chance in life. I wanted a good life away from the racism, judgment, and confusion of life in Arkansas. My teachers and guidance counselor wanted me to go to a college in Arkansas, but I had big dreams and my mind set to attend Harvard, Princeton, or Yale. I believed my mentor when he told me that "small liberal arts colleges" would give me scholarships. I had never heard of small liberal arts colleges. I did not know about the SAT, ACT, and the Profile.

Also, I was afraid that I would destroy the whole program if I told anyone. I would cause all of us to lose this opportunity, the connections, and information that so many of us black kids did not know we needed to succeed, to "get in." He held the keys to the kingdom, and I felt all alone in keeping the doors of opportunity open for all of us. I convinced myself that maybe I just imagined it; maybe it won't happen again; maybe I was overreacting.

One day, a hall monitor at my high school found me wandering aimlessly on the school campus. I was in a haze and unaware of how I got anywhere. Inside, I was sick, empty, broken, and numb.

The hall monitor brought me to the guidance counselor's office. There I sat, the straight-A, all-Honors, teacher's pet who preferred to stay at home with a tall stack of books. I had never been kissed, never had a boyfriend, never went to a school dance because I didn't know how to dance and felt intimidated at all the flirting and moving.

My grades had plummeted, and I was skipping class. I had stopped eating and survived on Ritz crackers and honey that I ate on the way to school. No one understood what was wrong. I didn't know how to explain what was wrong. Everything in me was shut down.

Chapter 2 Summary

- I was a smart black girl who grew up in a home where anything about the body, sex, or sovereignty was prohibited.
- Being inquisitive and questioning got me in trouble at home.
- My college preparatory mentor molested me, leaving me broken, numb, devastated, and depressed.

Chapter 3

A HEALING JOURNEY

> *My love, who told you the journey would be straight? Who told you that you would understand every step along the way? Give me a drink of that healing water. Let me bathe and rest my heart upon it.*

While every woman's story is unique, sadly, there are often similarities in what we experience in our lives. The pathways to reclaiming our lives, bodies, and spirits are as diverse as our stories. I want to share this path that led me out of the darkness, and that has since helped many other people with whom I have had the privilege to work. I want to share how I learned to be a black woman who loves my body, embraces my rich, unconventional life, and creates joy, celebration, pleasure, and power, despite circumstances that indicated otherwise.

Again, I reiterate that this kind of healing is available to you, no matter your ethnicity, body type, ability, or life circumstance. I'm sharing something that everyone, including you, can have access to.

The group of adults in the office told me that I had to drop an honors class and take an elective. Dance or choir, they said.

"You're working too hard. You're stressing yourself out."

I just nodded absently and chose dance.

I know now that dance chose me. Fate chose me. Divine love chose me.

Dance was a new program at my high school. I enrolled in the second semester, so I skipped the technique classes and went straight to creativity and experimentation. This was an absolute blessing. I was in no shape to learn anything or listen to another adult instructing me.

Our first assignment was to create a solo. We had complete creative license: any music, any genre. It could be anything we wanted, as long as it was at least one minute long.

A few weeks later, it was time to show our dances. We performed for our class of about 25 students in the theater lobby. The floor was a cream-colored, slick marble that reflected the overhead fluorescent lights. It was very cold to our bare feet. We made a semi-circle stage for the dancers and shared our solos.

Most of the girls had dance training and created beautiful, lyrical, jazzy, or hip-hop dances. I didn't have any training. I just had myself and more emotional turmoil than I could ever explain.

My turn came. The teacher pressed play on the CD player, and the haunting melody of "Deliver Us," from The Prince of Egypt soundtrack, echoed through the lobby.

I walked slowly and regally across the makeshift stage to the mournful sound of the trumpet, my arms spread out, chest up, confidently embracing the horn's sorrowful tune. I took a deep breath and let the sound wash over me as I paced, my heart thumping with fear and exhilaration. This was my first dance solo, and it was coming straight from my 16-year-old soul.

With a loud pop!, a whip snapped, and violin bows tore across the strings, causing my back to arch and then bend low, first trudging and stomping; jerking and tearing at myself till I crashed, scrambling on the slick floor. I cowed in a tight ball, the cold marble against my forehead, hot breath making moisture on the ground as my breath rushed in and out of my lungs.

I was moved to tears when I saw this scene in the movie: the struggle, ceaseless hope, and triumph of the slaves of Egypt. The song reflected the internal battle I was experiencing: how to be myself, speak my truth, and live in the world powerfully and on my terms. I never knew I had a choice until now.

"Deliver us!" The choir roared, and violins soared, mirroring me as I ran, twirled, and thrust. I undulated softly to my knees, my spine liquid, sweeping my hands wide, caressing my curves and skin in rhythm with the hushed whisper of the flute and a woman's croon. Suddenly, the singer's voice crescendoed with an ululation, both infinitely desolate and exquisitely hopeful. I felt myself as a budding flower, puncturing through cold white snow, a defiant proclamation of life.

I had never felt such freedom of expression, such pure connection to myself. I danced for three life-changing minutes. In those three minutes, I embodied and released all the rage, pain, shame, and confusion that resided inside and poisoned me. In that dance, with the big orchestral music and the lyrics saying, "Deliver us out of bondage to the land that you promised us," I felt my body. My promised land was my own body, my heart, my soul. I moved with wild abandon, slow grace, and punctuated precision. I cried, I breathed, and I groaned. I touched my own body. I moved my body how I wanted to move it. I reclaimed myself as my own. And I had witnesses.

This dance marked the beginning of my journey, which became my purpose—a purpose that I knew I had to share with the world. I had suffered at the hands of my mentor and the imprisonment of myself. I well know the confusion of being a dark-skinned girl in the south, at navigating the confines of religion, history, culture, and societal expectations that did not have me, my safe, beautiful, human self, in mind.

My gift to the world is to guide others toward finding the gift of themselves, of loving their bodies, walking in their power, and embracing their unique expression and joy.

This is a reclamation of the intelligence that our society has lost and buried. This intelligence would have empowered me to speak up, would have given my mentor an embodied sense of boundaries, consent, respect, honoring of my body and his, and so much more.

Gathering the Pieces

Dance was just the tip of the iceberg. Over the years, I continued the deep work, healing myself of the negative and disempowering stories I had learned to direct toward myself. I received the best training: a mix of traditional healing modalities and unconventional life experiences, all of which allowed me to become joyful and integrated with my body, expression, and pleasure in a world that is systematically designed to squash them.

I studied sociology and dance at Pomona College and developed an understanding of the body as both a social scientist and an artist. I have always loved observing people's complexities and quirks. Let's face it: people are weird. Sociology provided a methodical, scientific, yet humanist way to approach the study of our behavior.

After college, I became a performance artist, and when I moved to the San Francisco Bay Area, I got connected to the queer performing arts scene. Being in this community was a gift because I experienced creating transformational art. We unapologetically pushed the envelope and crafted an environment where we could express, love, be weird, and be heard. We shared the journey of finding oneself and daring to be authentic and wild despite the restrictions of dominant narratives.

Art is a laboratory for being fully human because it is a container that provides a safe place to push beyond the boundaries of who we think we are, to who we actually can become.

The juxtaposition of my studies in sociology and dance encouraged me to approach my own life and the work I do with a fresh lens: life is both an art and a science. We need in-depth study and structure, but we also need play and wonder.

I also studied conscious sexuality, took sex-educator training, became certified as a yoga instructor and an intimacy and relationship counselor. I wanted to open my eyes and heal the unconscious patterns around my body and my relationships. I knew there was a deeper inquiry I needed to explore to empower myself. I had already experienced first-hand the damage caused by ignorance and silence.

My transition away from being shame-filled, terrified of my own body, and oblivious of my powers was gradual and is ongoing. Every experience is an opportunity to examine how I lost myself, the impact this loss made on my life, and how to find those vital pieces again. My journey is not that of a scholar but one an adventurer. I committed to living an intuitive, resourced, and examined life with the guidance of my mentors.

I get to share my personal experiences and professional training with people who have felt the call for more: more connection, more freedom, more pleasure, more energy, and vitality. I've had the honor of mentoring and facilitating embodiment, Sensual Intelligence, and authentic expression for teachers, doctors, corporate professionals, entrepreneurs, social workers, ballerinas, sex workers, and more.

No matter the label, Sensual Intelligence work is about guiding us to reclaim ourselves, our power, and our gifts so that we can rewrite our story. We learn to treat our bodies with reverence and respect and finally understand what it means to be fully, joyfully human.

My story is not new. It is not unique. Everything that led up to the moment of my molestation and everything that occurred afterward—my ignorance about my own body, power dynamics, cultural taboos, societal expectations, and rules—are the same things that have influenced many people's lives.

The structure of our society is missing an integral piece. That void leaves us internally divided, disconnected from ourselves and each other. We see the outcomes of this internal dissonance in social and political issues like #Metoo, Black Lives Matter, police brutality, loneliness, the quality of our intimate relationships, and how we navigate our professional world. The reality is that most of us are missing the key ingredient to knowing and loving ourselves fully.

That missing piece is the lost IQ: Sensual Intelligence.

Chapter 3 Summary

- I reclaimed my body, power, voice, and expression through a solo dance I created at school.
- This started my journey of leading others to have empowered relationships with their bodies and sensuality.
- Our society is missing an integral piece that has led to a lot of ignorance and hurt in our development as individuals and society.
- That missing piece is Sensual Intelligence.

Chapter 4

KNOW YOUR DESTINATION – DEFINING SENSUAL IQ

My bible is a book of pleasures.
Of open mouths and heads thrown back,
the long strands of my twisted curls touching, tickling, stroking your chest, cheek, ears, as I
K
 I
  S
   S
    D
     O
   W
N
your body.
I turn the page.
Feeling the whisper of your lips against mine, as we speak the words of God,
Words of divination from my lips to yours, and yours to mine and back.
We are holy.
We are Whole.
We are wholly whole.

In that moment of freedom during my first dance performance, I caught a glimpse of the possibility of a different world. It would take me many years of practice, many setbacks, and much soul-searching until I could fully comprehend and describe to others what, exactly, I had found. In this chapter, I'll share this understanding with you. Since there is no singular way we all understand things, I will try various approaches to define Sensual Intelligence.

Sensual Intelligence – An existential definition

Sensual Intelligence is the embodied, artful knowledge of feeling and being. It is our ability to understand, discern, and appreciate the part of us that is sensitive, alive, and feeling.

It exists wherever our bodies exist, in all the body's expressions. It manifests as a feeling of joy, wonder, and connection in our bodies' expressions. Sensual Intelligence is the art of being connected to our human experience. It is mind, heart, and body integration.

In other words, Sensual Intelligence is the intelligence of our bodies in relationship with ourselves, others, and our environment. It is the ability to be present, consciously and creatively interacting with ourselves and the world. It is important because it shapes the quality of how we live our lives.

So many of us feel a deep, yearning hunger that we don't know how to fill. We try to satiate this hunger by checking off our bucket list items, getting into a relationship, landing the perfect job, buying that house, and thinking that we will feel fulfilled this time. Some of us feel thwarted by all of life's responsibilities and obligations, and we are worn out and crushed. Others find solace in numbness, having too long deferred the dreams of joy, satisfaction, pleasure, ecstasy, and wonder.

Much of this sense of deprivation is a consequence of a Sensual Intelligence deficit. It's not the things we do or achieve, not what we own or buy, nor the roles we play in life that define joy and fulfillment—it is how we do the things and play the roles. Living with presence and consciousness, with a capacity for joy, motivates and drives creation.

However, when we feel like we don't have permission to explore ourselves, what we like, what feels good to us, what feels toxic, we default to what we are told should be fulfilling. The journey of reclaiming Sensual Intelligence is a journey to wholeness, bringing together body, mind, and heart as a way of being in, experiencing, and creating our world in a way that optimizes our human potential.

Sensual IQ is a felt intelligence, one that fills our world with living poetry and invites us to embody the beautiful essence of life. It feels like an elixir of joy, like a "spiritual facelift," as one client has described it.

> *After a deep practice of clearing fear and shame that she held in her body around her beauty, one client described her experience in this way:*
>
> *"I didn't know how to rekindle my sensual expression beyond performing for others. It didn't feel like it was mine anymore. Recently, I've been exploring my sensual connection from such a pure space. All the energy we cleared in my body showed up as a primal power and an ability to move with my breath in such an intense and powerful way. I felt so much space in my body since we worked together. It's revolutionary. All of the heavy pressure, compression, this weight, this density around my heart has cleared. It feels like a wide-open space now in my whole body, my whole essence. It moves through my heart. There's this freedom, a beautiful field of flowers in my heart." ~ Daria*

Transforming our relationship with our bodies and sensuality is a humbling experience. The pathway to feeling safe and at home in our bodies occurs through a metamorphosis where we find parts of ourselves that we didn't know existed.

Speed and Spice: Sensuality is NOT Sex

Imagine you're suddenly in possession of a gorgeous, sleek sports car. It waits for you outside, all aerodynamic lines and powerful, engineering perfection. You immediately jump in, turn on the engine, and put the pedal to the metal, launching from 0–60 in no time! "Whew, that was great," you say as you come to a sudden stop. You decide to go to the grocery store. Bam!, 0–60 mph. You go visit your friend a mile away. Wham!, 0–60 mph. Everywhere you go, no matter how far away, when your foot hits the accelerator, you are a fast, hard blur of metal and rubber.

However, there are consequences for you, the neighborhood, and the vehicle itself with this unrelenting throttle to optimum speed. Your hair becomes disheveled. You may develop a slightly jittery disposition from constantly subjecting your body to rocket speeds. You're definitely a menace to your neighborhood because it is inevitable that you will endanger others. And the car itself will quickly wear out.

This is how most of us have been taught about sensuality. Through word, deed, advertising rules, and beyond, the first thing that comes to mind when we hear the word sensual is sex. We learn that sensuality is just another word for sex. At the very least, we assume that sensuality will eventually culminate in sex.

News flash. This may just blow your mind.

Sensuality is not sexuality. Sensuality does not lead to sex. It is not sex. Sensuality is not another word for sex. Sensual Intelligence is not about teaching sex. SENSuality comes from your SENSory system—it's all about noticing the feelings in your body and living in a way that is informed by them. The way we have been taught to experience sensuality is the equivalent of the sports car story I shared above.

Don't get me wrong, there is nothing wrong with sex. I LOVE sex—a lot. But let me make this plain and simple: sex is NOT the same as sensuality, and sensuality is not exclusive to sex.

Sensuality supports sex, and sex can be (and should be, in my humble opinion) sensual, but they are not the same thing. By increasing your SQ, you will be more likely to get sexual fulfillment because you will be more open and sensitive to yourself, your partner(s), and the world around you. This sensitivity is like painting with a full-color palette or cooking with a full spice rack, creating a deep, rich, tasty experience of life.

I went to a birthday party where they played a game dipping chicken wings into progressively potent hot sauces. There were tears, dry heaving, much milk gulping, and more than one out-of-body experience by the end of the game. After the spice competition had ended, one person came late to the party and unwittingly helped himself to a hefty scoop of one of the hottest sauces. His roar of pain as he sprinted, red-faced and sweating, to the kitchen faucet was hilarious for the onlookers and horrible for his stomach lining.

Sensuality is like pepper and spice. If someone told you to eat a pepper, you'd want to know what kind of pepper it is because you know that every pepper will give you a different experience. The same goes for sensuality. Sensuality is really the whole spectrum of spice, not just the hottest. You wouldn't want every meal to be laden with the hottest of peppers. Your palette yearns for the sensual variety and information of the softest caresses, the most abrasive strokes, and everything in between.

As long as we conflate sex and sensuality, we will never know what life experiences are available. Without Sensual Intelligence, we will treat all sensuality like jalapeños or Carolina Reapers: thrilling but dangerous. This gross oversimplification causes us to lose out on many gifts of having a body. The whole range of experiences is what is essential.

SQ has not been consistently, consciously taught, or practiced for most of us. Therefore, it is no surprise that our interactions can be awkward and filled with misunderstandings, mistakes, and confusion. You cannot expect to have mastery and dexterity in something with which you do not have a relationship. With Sensual Intelligence practices, you can refine your relationship and perception of yourself and others.

In Chapter 24—Intimacy, Eros, and Relationships—we will dive into how to cultivate Sensual Intelligence in your intimate relationships. I put it at the end of the book because everything you need to enjoy erotic connection is found in all the practices I share throughout our journey.

If deeply satisfying sexual pleasure is what brought you here, I want to leave you with this one word: foreplay. Everything leading up to our conversation about sex is foreplay at its finest. So go through this journey with me, and I will show you how to have an entire life of orgasmic pleasure and connection.

Sensual Intelligence Practice (SIP)

With that in mind, I want to introduce you to SIP, Sensual Intelligence Practices. These are guided activities that will help build your Sensual Intelligence. They are scattered throughout this book, and I encourage you to do them. The tricky thing about sensuality is that you can't get sensual intelligence by just reading this book. It's not osmosis. You have to do the work and be in the experience. You will have to do weird things like move your body, make noises, talk to yourself, ask yourself questions that you've never considered, journal, and more.

We are a world full of differently-abled bodies, and Sensual Intelligence is for all bodies, even if your body has different abilities. If your body cannot do some activities precisely as I describe, that's OK. Simply modify to fit your body's capabilities, and do as much as you can physically. What you cannot physically do, hold a powerful intention, and perform the activity in your mind. Your attention to your body and your intention behind the practice will make all the difference.

Let's try this together.

SIP
(Sensual Intelligence Practice)

I have led this chant to audiences big and small, professional and intimate, getting people stomping, clapping, smiling, and in their bodies, activating the connection of mind, body, and heart, with themselves and their community. It is inspired by the church where I grew up, where we did call-and-response chants. Imagine saying these words in an embodied community, everyone with one heartbeat, one breath. The body movements and voice vibrations amplify the words so that they reverberate inside your very cells. This is an embodied experience, not just something in the mind.

Stand up.
Say this chant out loud three times, increasing your volume and movement each time.

I am Power
Hear me roar
I love my body
So I can soar.
I know my mind
Ideas so bright.
I speak from my heart
And shine my light.

Take a moment now, and feel your body. Feel your heartbeat, feel the breath as it goes in and out of your body. This pause to feel your own body is the first step toward feeling the potency of Sensual Intelligence, the lost art of feeling and being alive.

Chapter 4 Summary

- Sensual Intelligence is the embodied, artful knowing of feeling and being.
- It is the intelligence of our bodies in relationship with ourselves and others.
- Sex and sensuality are not mutually exclusive. Sensuality exists along a spectrum.
- Sensual Intelligence has not been taught, and this limits our ability to express ourselves.
- SIP (Sensual Intelligence Practices) are guided practices that will increase SQ. Do them.

Chapter 5

HOW DID WE LOSE IT?

> ### The Fruit of Your Garden
>
> *Feel the sun on your skin and the wildness blossoming from your chest. Reclaim and cultivate your Garden of Eden. With every act of love, honor, generosity, and forgiveness; with every honest smile, laugh, and tickle; with every shared kiss and caress; with every act of love-making and conscious celebration of bodies joining; cultivate your garden.*
>
> *Dare to love yourself, show yourself, and share yourself, no matter what.*
> *Come. Sit. Be with yourself in your garden. Let your love and beauty nourish you so that you nourish others with your bounty.*
>
> *Your fruit is not forbidden; it is infinitely divine.*

I want to warn you that the following few pages will be intense. Every single part of this book, even the segments that feel uncomfortable, is integral to reclaiming our bodies, our power, and embodied joy. I will briefly share some of the things I've seen to be contributors to the loss of SQ. I'm not going to go into depth on these subjects because I want to keep us focused on the journey of reclaiming ourselves. But the path to wholeness necessarily has some truths that we must face.

Lean into the sensations that you may initially call discomfort, tightness, or an intrusion upon your peace. Engage with this feeling part of yourself. It is the most authentic call to action you will ever receive. When we make ourselves numb and cancel the sensuality, the Sensual Intelligence made available in the moments of most pain, disappointment, and despair, we miss an opportunity for a more profound knowledge of self.

Once upon a time, we were babies. Adults squeezed our chubby cheeks, stared into our large eyes, and called us "perfect." We touched ourselves and ate our toes. We explored and demanded our needs with piercing baby cries. We played and laughed with our entire bodies. We were open and full of wonder, raw and honest, using our bodies to explore and understand the world.

Under ideal circumstances, we would learn to develop this SQ along with IQ and EQ. We would master the dance of our sensual bodies, emotions, and cognitive abilities, so our bodies could be vessels of delight, learning, connection, and growth. We would mature into sovereign, yet interdependent people, contributing to and nourishing our relationships, communities, and environments.

However, things went a little bit differently. While we learned what is right and wrong, acceptable and forbidden, and how to function as contributors to society, we were not explicitly taught the skills for living in authenticity and joy.

American writer, poet, and cartoonist, Shel Silverstein, created "Thinker of Tender Thoughts," an illustration that drives this point home. The comic shows the time-lapse of a boy as he grows into a man. In each drawing, he gets older. Instead of hair, flowers grow from his head until, halfway through illustrations, he is an adult with a full bouquet of wild blossoms sprouting from his scalp. Then, in the next slide, he faces his friends, who all have identical close-shorn hairstyles, short as grass, without any blossoms. They point and laugh at his unruly flowers. Dejected, he turns away and leaves. In the next slide, he takes scissors and cuts the flowers from his head. They lie dead and strewn on the floor at his feet. In the final drawing, we see that he has returned to join his friends, whom he now exactly resembles.

We go through some version of this every day of our lives, especially after childhood. It is the journey of the loss of Sensual Intelligence, the loss of self and innocence.

Our histories, familial relationships, cultures, and societal expectations have taught us how to see and be with our bodies. But unfortunately, the same conditioning that taught us how to achieve success in society led us to disconnect from our authentic, fully integrated selves.

Detaching from our bodies, labeling emotions as inferior, and glorifying cognitive intelligence is the path to losing Sensual Intelligence. And it is not solely an individual occurrence. It is rooted in history.

"All men are created equal."

The combined forces of toxic, short-sighted patriarchy and colonialism lead to our particular loss of Sensual Intelligence. I emphasize the word *toxic* because any form of governance and societal structure has the potential for toxicity. Toxicity simply means an imbalanced, unchecked, not adaptive response to the needs and health of a population. History shows us time and again that social systems fail when there is too much imbalance, no matter who is considered in charge. Keep this in mind as we move forward. It is so easy to fall into the same patterning of blaming, shaming, and punishing each other, rather than truly learning to adapt to the natural complexities of our humanity. For us right now, the legacy of colonialism, supremacy, and patriarchal American society taught us to be disempowered and disconnected from our bodies.

> *The ones who write history determine our perceived reality; but if we choose to listen to the root wisdom of our bodies, then we rewrite our stories and create our authentic, embodied reality.*

The following passage is written history.

"We hold these truths to be self-evident, that all men are created equal, that they are endowed by their Creator with certain unalienable Rights, that among these are Life, Liberty and the pursuit of Happiness.—That to secure these rights, Governments are instituted among Men, deriving their just powers from the consent of the governed[...][1]

These words in the Declaration of Independence are a beautiful idea. If you look at the definition of Sensual Intelligence, you will see that they share some of the same language and ideology.

"Sensual Intelligence is the embodied, artful knowledge of feeling and being. It is our ability to understand, discern, and appreciate the part of us that is sensitive, alive, and feeling[...]

It manifests as a feeling of joy, wonder, and connection in our bodies' expressions. Sensual Intelligence is the art of being connected to our human experience."

The "unalienable Rights" of "Life, Liberty, and the pursuit of Happiness" is the same as the "feeling of joy, wonder, and connection in our bodies' expressions." Oh, and I love the use of the word consent! "Deriving their just powers from the consent of the government" is terrific, especially if you understand the *embodied* definition of the word consent, which I explain in detail in Chapter 15. But, for now, let me give you a little hint: you can't have consent without being sensual.

---

[1] The Declaration of Independence.
https://www.archives.gov/founding-docs/declaration-transcript

The thing about words is that they are only as accurate as their sensual embodied actions. Otherwise, they're just placeholders of ideas, with no tangible efforts to make them real.

Let's take the first line of the Declaration of Independence, and see how the words align with sensual embodied reality.

"[A}ll men are created equal, that they are endowed by their Creator with certain unalienable Rights, that among these are Life, Liberty and the pursuit of Happiness."

We cannot separate the success of America from the starkly unequal treatment of humans. First of all, slavery and indigenous genocide are the foundation of this country's success. Stripping the value from the human body, forcing black and brown men, women, and children to disown themselves and forfeit their bodies, sovereignty, dignity, lifeblood, culture, and humanity for the profitable gain of others, was the embodied reality. No one can pursue life, liberty, and happiness if they are punished for being in the body they are in; penalized for being connected to their body's autonomy and pleasure. This is literally in direct violation of sensual intelligence. There is no way a society whose very values are built upon empty promises and slave labor can have kept Sensual Intelligence and justice for all.

Even if we are only the descendants of these crimes, these power dynamics shaped our ancestors, which shaped family dynamics, which shaped communities, which shaped cities, nations, and a culture.

Humans develop in communities; our communities create our culture; our culture creates our rules of engagement and the pulse of society. Sociology teaches us that people use everyday interactions to create a common-sense view of the world. Societal rules are social constructs made through adherence to social contracts, implicit and explicit. The legacy left by this systemic trauma is, in large part, what led to whole populations being disinherited from accessing sensual intelligence, generation to generation. No one came out unscathed, whether knowledgeable perpetrators, unwitting participants, ignorant bystanders, or direct victims.

We're at war. We're at war with the narratives of our bodies. We're waging war against the earth and our very humanity. Colonization never stopped. We just turned it toward ourselves. Once colonized, the rules of colonization must be enforced to keep the system in place, and the mascots for colonization are profit and productivity.

Productivity is the pride of American culture. Many people find their value in how much they produce and how fast they can deliver. There is a constant fear of not doing enough and being judged as lazy, unsuccessful, and unambitious. The message is to be driven, ambitious, and success-oriented. "Grab that bag!" "Get on the grind!" "Crush it!" "Kill it!" "Nailed it!"

It is no mistake that this language is prevalent in the workspace, especially arenas where productivity is the law. It is commonplace to be slammed by work and hang on by tooth and nail using your blood, sweat, and tears. These messages permeate everyday life, driving people to push their bodies to the point of exhaustion, adrenal fatigue, and total burnout. Our legacy of toxic patriarchy and colonialism is so ingrained that these symptoms of dis-ease are considered normal, everyday life. Our world was designed to overload our senses so that we have to filter things out and go numb.

Part of our journey as a society is recognizing that this loss of Sensual Intelligence is historical and cultural, not just a result of individual practices and modern society. I believe our most significant change will come from embracing pleasure as a culture.

While the results of the trauma of colonization manifest in different ways, the healing process is the same: heal the body, heal our connection to the body, heal the collective body. We learn how to create safe spaces for ourselves to heal our wounds around the body, sensuality, and emotional expression. We do not change the world by participating in it under the same rules and structures in which it was created. We recreate it with a whole new structure, a structure in which we connect to our bodies and generate ease within our hearts and minds.

Gender

Now, let's look at the loss of SQ through gender and gender limitations. For people who are labeled women, the toxicity reveals itself when we are told that developing the wisdom of our body, pleasure, and claiming sovereignty is wrong and dangerous. It is not considered OK for women to be too beautiful, outspoken, independent, and vocal. We learn to be "good girls," which means we have to forfeit our self-expression and have weak personal boundaries. Or, if we dare stand our ground, they risk being a "bitch," "too much," "out of her place."

For people who are labeled men, the toxicity reveals itself when they learn that their body is solely a place of prowess, power, weaponization, sexual dominance, and emotionless fortitude. Children gendered as boys are told they must be physically strong and competitive, emotionally stoic, or aggressive. We treat their vulnerability and need for affection as unimportant or non-existent. They have freedom but are left to fend for themselves emotionally. Boys end up inheriting a stark future void of sweetness and softness.

From Eve in the Garden of Eden to Pandora's Box, the message is clear: bad things happen when people access Sensual Intelligence. To explore the joyful, life-giving intelligence of your body is to eat the forbidden fruit.

It doesn't have to be this way. Dr. Clarissa Pinkola Estés, author of *Women Who Run With the Wolves*, wrote an incredible book that takes readers on an archetypal journey to reclaim women's bodies and power. Through the stories and myths, we see that women are more than just venerated, voluptuous vessels of fertility, hearth, and abundance. The feminine is so much more. It is fierce, free, and wild.

We need to look at the origin stories of toxic masculinity and what social, emotional, mental, and community resources we need to heal this deep, disruptive wounding. Hint: It's not the sole responsibility for men to change. There are deep-seated imbalances in the rearing of boys (and children in general) that lead to so much of the behavior we call toxic.

This needs to be taught in the classroom and beyond. Update the definition of the feminine and the masculine to include the complex qualities that are both nurturing and ferocious. "Masculine" and "feminine" are not limited to particular bodies. Instead, they are qualities of expression and being that *all* bodies can do. *All* bodies have a spectrum of masculine and feminine qualities because that's just human.

Love, affection, and belonging are basic human necessities. Perceived gender should not determine the love we receive and express. We all need to feel that we belong and are safe. Belonging is not something static that we force-fit ourselves into. Belonging is an ever-evolving process. Just because something seems different doesn't mean it is dangerous; it's just a part of our evolutionary journey.

The practice of Sensual Intelligence is a revolutionary act. It starts from the inside, with healing ourselves and our bodies, granting permission, and allowing ourselves to feel and reconnect to our very humanity, our bodies' ability to see, connect, feel, and create beauty and nourishment. Practicing Sensual Intelligence is all about breaking the cycle of disenfranchisement.

There is no perfect path, and there is no shame when you get started on this journey. But, we can initiate these needed conversations and develop embodied practices in safe, trusted, loving communities with knowledgeable facilitators. Together, we can work toward healing and change. We can learn how to live our best, most fulfilled lives through sensual intelligence practices. We have to start somewhere, and hopefully, this book can help.

Chapter 5 Summary
- The very foundation of capitalism and the American industrial machine is in the dehumanization and de-sensualization of humans.
- We have separated mind, body, and heart. We have numbed our bodies and feelings to be productive.
- The body cannot help but remember its natural state of freedom, even if it must express itself unconsciously.
- Living in discord with our own bodies' intelligence contributes to diseases, mental illness, and family conflict.

Chapter 6

WHO IS SMART?

When most of us think of IQ, we think of standardized tests that measure how "smart" we are. The resulting number is a badge some people wear proudly, which can open doors if it is high enough, like the exclusive Mensa Club of super-smart people. However, what has been called the IQ should more accurately be called Cognitive IQ. This specific intelligence is associated with learning, remembering, reasoning, solving problems, and making sound judgments. But there are serious flaws with looking at IQ, i.e., Cognitive Intelligence, in isolation because of the implications of its origins.

My grandfather, Dr. Robert L. Williams, author, professor at Washington University, and thought leader (he coined the term 'ebonics'), created the BITCH-100 test, the Black Intelligence Test of Cultural Homogeneity, in 1972. It illuminated the bias of "standardized" tests.

He proposed that IQ tests were culturally biased and that he could prove it by creating a test that was skewed toward people who identify as Black. True to what he hypothesized, White people performed poorly, and Black people excelled in the BITCH-100 test. The IQ test, as it was written and administered before my grandfather's findings, resulted in Black people disproportionately performing poorly, and then being placed in Special Education classes. The Larry P. case was a prime example of this. It was a landmark case involving five African American students' families suing the school district for discrimination and unnecessary placement in what was then called "educable mentally retarded" (EMR) classes due to their IQ test scores. Dr. Robert L. Williams was an expert witness to overturning this practice.

The BITCH-100 test showed that the test questions and language were created through the lens of the dominant group, utilizing a very narrow range of what could be counted as a "high score." This provided proof that though the IQ test claimed to be an objective assessment method, IQ was actually a social construct, subject to favoritism. After these findings, the testing industry significantly increased the number of Black people in their norming samples (as there were none in the past), changing items to increase the cultural fairness of the IQ test.[2]

The state of California, to this day, prohibits Black children from being placed in special education solely due to IQ tests.[3] You may recall that I suffered from a similar kind of discrimination in my school in Arkansas. I did not take an IQ test before I was placed in Special Education classes; I simply "looked like" someone who should be in special education.

I share this story to point out the inherent biases around intelligence and ask deeper questions. What is considered smart? Who is valuable? Who creates what we value in society, and at what cost? The concept of IQ was socially constructed by a specific group that normalized their way of being as the appropriate way. The IQ test merely reified this power structure, further marginalizing and burying different kinds of intelligence. What are the consequences of this modus operandi?

While my grandfather created consciousness around the testing of intelligence with the BITCH Test-100, in 1995, Daniel Goleman published Emotional Intelligence, which, because it gained such popularity, changed how we think of human intelligence. Emotional Intelligence is our ability to

---

[2] R.A. Williams (personal communication, June 28, 2021). Dr. Robert A. Williams, Dean of the College of Education and Allied Studies at California State University East Bay, my Grandfather's seventh son, and my Uncle.

[3] You can find more information about this landmark case here: https://www.kqed.org/news/11781032/a-landmark-lawsuit-aimed-to-fix-special-ed-for-californias-black-students-it-didnt

perceive, integrate, understand, and regulate our emotions in a way that promotes personal growth.[4] Emotional Intelligence was more effective in predicting people's success in career and life. Yet, this intelligence was neither recognized nor valued because it did not fit into the capitalistic, patriarchal, colonial value system from which it originated.

Where Are We Smart?

Western science has almost exclusively focused on the brain to explain how humans develop and interact. This brain-centered explanation of biological human development traces our development from the oldest parts of the brain, located in the back, to the youngest parts, located in the front. The oldest part of the brain is made up of the brain stem and amygdala. These focus on primal instincts and survival. Next comes the limbic system, which is concerned with emotions and belonging. The frontal cortex comes next, which is the area of cognitive reasoning. Science then discovered the prefrontal cortex, which is the part of the brain that can create a web of connection among all aspects of the brain. Development of this part allows for our self-awareness, empathy, compassion, and connection to others.

However, most recent research confirms the intelligence found in the body itself, where literal bundles of neurons act independently and in cooperation with the brain. After all, our development starts in utero, where our bodies are awash in the blood, hormones, skin, and fluid of the womb. This body-to-body connection is where we obtain all of our initial information before making it out to the world. When we are born, our bodies continue to be the primary source of information absorption and processing. Developmentally, IQ isn't even on the table until we start to develop and use language.

In terms of science, Sensual Intelligence is concerned with this process: the process through which the intelligence of the body-brain, the gut-brain, the

---

[4] Daniel Goleman. Emotional Intelligence. New York: Bantam Books, 1995. Print.

heart brain, and the head brain all converge. Through this research, we will find the magic of Sensual Intelligence.

The body is a complex connection of systems. So too is our planet. It is composed of water, soil, plants, animals, fungi, all working together to form what we know as life on earth. We are a part of the system of life on the planet, and Sensual Intelligence takes this connection into account. Through the body's senses, we feel the sensuality of another being, our relationships, and our place in our environment and communities. Through Sensual Intelligence, we learn to connect with our bodies, our bodies' systems, and the wisdom of this body as it is connected to everything else. We realize that we are inextricably woven together.

Sensual Intelligence gives embodied answers on living in harmonic regeneration with our environment and creating supportive communities. There is no need for people to die of loneliness and ostracism because they don't know how to get their basic needs (like human touch and affection). Sensual Intelligence makes us stop and say, "Oh, I am that, and that is me," and actually feel it.

SQ is another step in the journey of claiming our entire intelligence and practicing a holistic way of being. It considers the reality of our sensual, sensing, sensate bodies, through which emotional intelligence and cognitive intelligence must filter, and vice versa. My primary motivation in writing this book is to draw attention to the inescapable truth that, despite our progress, we have not yet arrived at defining, valuing, and utilizing the multifaceted scope of human intelligence.

We are taking several significant steps in defining human intelligence to integrate a much broader and more accurate range of abilities. SQ and EQ are necessary responses to the structures that heavily rely on IQ. Sensual Intelligence considers that we are humans, with various cultural backgrounds, interacting with each other and our environment through sensual, embodied practices.

I titled this book The Lost IQ not just because Sensual Intelligence is a cute and trendy term. Instead, it contributes to the rhetoric around what we value and teach. IQ has been given excessive and exclusive importance, ignoring or marginalizing other contributing intelligence.

There are socio-cultural and geopolitical repercussions for sweeping the wisdom of Sensual Intelligence under the rug. As long we do not recognize the sensual body as vital, we stifle opportunities to fully understand our humanity, connection to this planet, and potential for healing, growth, and connection.

It will take time for this hypothesis to gain attention, be substantiated and validated through scientific discourse, and ultimately claim its rightful place. However, I firmly believe that we cannot wait for this to happen before enjoying our lives more fully. Therefore, I am offering this book as an initial guide to those who are as impatient as I am.

Chapter 6 Summary

- Sensual Intelligence (SQ), Cognitive Intelligence (IQ), and Emotional Intelligence (EQ) are all important in the understanding of human evolution.
- SQ is another step in the journey of claiming our full intelligence and practicing a holistic way of being. It considers the reality of our sensual, sensing, sensate bodies, through which emotional intelligence and cognitive intelligence are expressed.
- Exclusive reliance on IQ results from bias and creates more bias in who and what we see as intelligent.

Part 2:

RECLAIMING YOUR SENSUAL BODY

Chapter 7

LET'S GET SENSUAL

> The Surrender
>
> *Soft shadows dark as night*
> *Pull me into their obsidian arms*
> *While the light of the bright sun*
> *Sparkles a dance*
> *On the sweat of my skin.*
> *And I surrender*
> *My body surrenders*
> *My heart surrenders*
> *To Deep, Soft, Present, Love.*

Sensual Intelligence practice is the practice of bringing yourself to life in all areas so that you can feel the pulse of your efforts and the aliveness of your being. When we get stuck in struggling and suffering, we are often trying to force and think our way through rather than feel the embodied truth.

Sensual Intelligence is composed of the *Sensual Body* and the *Sensual Expressions*.

Sensual Body

The Sensual Body is the building block of Sensual Intelligence. These are found in our bodies, hearts, minds, and environments. The Sensual Body includes

Embodment: relationship with the body
Self-Love: relationship with our heart and emotions
Mindfulness: relationship with our mind and thoughts
Community: relationship with others and the environment

Embodiment (Body)

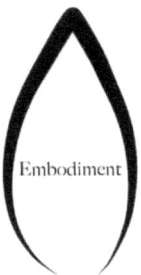

Sensual Intelligence is an embodied intelligence. It is found in and expressed through the body. Embodiment is not simply about having a body, it is *the level of awareness* in our bodies. Embodiment is our embodied awareness.

Body Awareness + Body Expression = Embodiment (Embodied Awareness)

Embodiment (embodied awareness) is measured through our ability to access our senses, to be present in, perceive, and express our physical selves. The degree to which we have embodied awareness is the degree to which we are conscious of what, how, and why our bodies are communicating, both to ourselves and others.

Lack of embodied awareness can make being in our bodies feel scary and uncomfortable. We may feel disconnected or that our body is betraying us. It can also make communicating with others and reading body communication confusing and awkward.

When we are consciously embodied, we feel comfortable in our bodies and expression. We can use our bodies to bring us joy and connection. We go into the journey of embodiment healing in Chapters 10 and 11.

Self-Love (Heart)

Self-Love is the ability to love and honor one's self. It consists of Self-Intimacy and Self-Acceptance.

Self-Intimacy + Self-Acceptance + Self-Integration = Self-Love

Self-Intimacy is the ability to be close with yourself, be in a close relationship with your inner, emotional world, and see yourself face-to-face. Self-Acceptance is the process by which we sit with and embrace what we see in ourselves, not with judgment, but with openness and presence. Self-Integration brings you a harmonious flow with your various emotions and life experiences. Self-Love is neither narcissistic nor self-indulgent. It is learning to see, accept, and celebrate who you are; your needs, wants, desires, and intentions. Self-Love invites you to integrate your heart and feelings.

It is important to note that even people with an excellent mind-body connection can lack essential Self-Love. Self-love is the journey of loving yourself so thoroughly that your love overflows onto others. When you realize the precious gift you are and feel it deep in your soul, you cannot help but see the beauty, humor, and divinity inside every other person's body.

Self-Love is an alchemical process that requires vulnerability. We are required to look deeply into ourselves, our values, and what we genuinely want to create in this world. We cannot give and receive love in a sustainable and regenerative way if we are not first intimate with ourselves (our emotional body and our heart) and then move into self-acceptance and self-integration. We explore the journey of self-love in Chapter 12.

Mindfulness (Mind)

Mindfulness is the role of the mind in Sensual Intelligence.

Mind's Natural Abilities + Awareness Practice = Mindfulness

We already view the mind, the brain, as the most important feature of our humanity. (I will be using the words mind and brain interchangeably). Yet, many people over the years have told me, "I want to get out of my head"! This is because the mind is not concerned about whether or not we thrive and enjoy life. Its job is to keep us safe and alive. As far as the brain is concerned, if we're alive, then we are winning. It doesn't matter if the quality of our lives is terrible.

In Sensual Intelligence, we use mindfulness to bring awareness to the mind's natural abilities: making thoughts, beliefs, habits, and judgments. Left unchecked, our thoughts make us prisoners in our heads, obsessing, criticizing, and limiting our potential. Mindfulness is a tool that helps discern which thoughts and judgments align with our thriving rather than knee-jerk survival habits.

The mindfulness journey can appear to be the most counter-intuitive in this expedition of Sensual Intelligence. However, we are retraining the mind by tapping into the body's wisdom. We use embodied awareness to train mindfulness (mind awareness). The interplay of mindfulness and embodiment fosters internal harmony that enlivens our sensual exploration.

In Chapter 13, we will explore how mindfulness contributes to Sensual Intelligence.

The Sensual Body and the Individual Journey

A big part of the Sensual Intelligence journey is our ability to know and connect with our Sensual Body. Embodiment, Self-Love, and Mindfulness make up the Sensual Body and focus on self-knowledge and self-awareness. Who we are for ourselves has a real impact on others. As long as we do not have an intimate relationship with ourselves, body, mind, and heart, we cannot access full growth and connection with others.

A lotus flower petal represents each aspect of the Sensual Body. The lotus is a plant that roots itself deep in the dark muck but then emerges as an incredibly bright, beautiful flower. So too is our personal journey: to grow and reach our full potential and beauty, we must go into the deep, into the dark parts of the sensual body.

The petals overlap, indicating the interconnected nature of ourselves. The body influences the mind, which influences the heart, which influences the body, in a dazzling swirl of life and growth.

The spiral at the bottom of the lotus represents the cycle of life; birth, growth, death, and reincarnation. The spiral will be a repeating visual symbol throughout because the road to self-knowledge and transformation is never straight, especially the path of sensual intelligence. It curves into itself, every experience giving us a different vantage and offering the opportunity to evolve and blossom.

Community (Environment)

We come to the final element of the Sensual Body: Community. The first three components of the Sensual Body are all about how we, as embodied *individuals*, experience and know ourselves. Community centers around our interconnected relationships with *others* and the environment.

Other Bodies + Environment = Community

No person is an island. A collection of individuals and the spaces we live in compose Community. Who we are for ourselves influences the Community we make and vice versa. Community is both a mirror that reflects us and an active agent that shapes us. Achieving harmony within our mind, body, and heart is a beautiful state, but only once we learn to interact with the world does it begin to give us the full value we seek.

The illustration of Community has plant arms, and the cupped human hands seamlessly merged, symbolizing an inseparable, collaborative alliance between nature and humanity. We are nature, and nature is us.

The Collective Journey

Sensual Intelligence is the coherent connection of mind-body-heart (the sensual body) in a community. We create our world from our inner, embodied experience. We are the lotus flower, daring the journey of self-discovery, held in the arms of the environment. The more disconnected we are from ourselves, including our sensuality, the more disconnected we are from each other and the environment. Healthy, integrated SQ makes us good stewards of ourselves, our relationships, and our relationship with our planet.

SIP
Journaling Exercise: Getting Honest with Yourself

I recommend doing this, and all journal prompts, with a physical journal and a pen. It allows you to connect with your body more intimately than using a screen.

We cannot change what we are unwilling or unable to witness. So take a moment to get honest with yourself. Grab yourself a cup of tea, some pillows, and set up a quiet place to sit with yourself.

Take your time.
Breathe.

- What is your relationship with your body, mind, heart, and community?
- Is it helpful or hurtful?
- Describe the last time you opened up to feeling joyful experience of yourself.
- What do you think keeps you trapped, disempowered, or numb?
- What areas do you feel uncomfortable in your body or another's body, and get stuck in your head.
- What would change if you felt joyful, expansive, at choice, and able to explore the depths of yourself?

Just breathe. There is no need to go back and read it. There is no need to judge what you've written. Be open to the doors of awareness

Sensual Expressions – The 7Ps

The 7Ps of Sensual Expression are how we express ourselves through our Sensual Bodies. The Sensual Body is the 'what,' while the Sensual Expressions are the 'how' we conduct, fuel, and motivate ourselves. The 7Ps are Pleasure, Play, Passion, Peace, Psyche, Power, and Philosophy. The characteristics of the Sensual Expressions are based on the elements. Pleasure is earth, Play is air, Passion is fire, Psyche is spirit, Philosophy is space, Power is metal, and Peace is water.

Everyone has all 7Ps of Sensual Expression; however, we all have a different level of connectedness with each one. Our unique blend of the 7Ps accounts for our different sensual strengths and expressions.

SENSUAL INTELLIGENCE

Element: Earth

Qualities: Sensual, present, lush

Sensual Intelligence Type: The Sensualist

Pleasure is the expression of the body's joys and delights. It invites us to slow down and savor the present moment.

Element: Air

Qualities: Playful, lighthearted, visionary

Sensual Intelligence Type: The Creative

Play is the expression of curiosity and exploration. It is connected to the inner child and it speaks to the lightness of spirit and the qualities of wonder, imagination, and joy.

Element: Fire

Qualities: Expressive, emotive, catalyst

Sensual Intelligence Type: The Diva

Passion is the expression of movement and aliveness. It is the fire of the heart, unapologetically lighting the path of internal truth.

Element: Metal

Qualities: Structured and clear boundaries, decisive, meticulous

Sensual Intelligence Type: The Domme

Power is the expression of boundaries and structure. It is the journey of sovereignty, and how we claim and occupy space.

Element: Spirit

Qualities: Transcendent, wise, mysterious

Sensual Intelligence Type: The Mystic

Psyche is the expression of spirit. It is concerned with energy, the unseen, ethereal, and omnipresent. It experiences the sacred connection of all things.

Element: Space

Qualities: Scientific, curious, proof, and data-driven

Sensual Intelligence Type: The Intellect

Philosophy is the expression of research, knowledge, and truth. It is concerned with the understanding, testing, and proving of things.

Peace

Element: Water

Qualities: Flowing, nourishing, nurturing

Sensual Intelligence Type: The Empath

Peace is the expression of love and acceptance. It is the nourishing softness that creates safety, trust, and connection.

Life happens. We get hurt. We're used to seeing and dealing with injuries on the physical body. If we break a leg, we go to a doctor and get it set and immobilized with a splint and cast. We hobble around awkwardly on crutches, letting the limb mend while the rest of the body compensates for this loss in mobility. However, *Sensual* Body injuries often go unrecognized and untreated. Trauma, shame, and conditioning are injuries to our Sensual Body. For example, being continuously told, "Boys don't cry. Suck it up, crybaby!" after your feelings have been hurt is a trauma done to the Sensual Body.

Why is this important?

Everyone has all 7Ps of Sensual Expression; each of the 7Ps is part of a complete, interdependent system, just like our physical body. But most of us do not have access to all of our expressions because we are compensating for untreated Sensual Body injuries.

An injury to one part affects the whole. If left unchecked or improperly tended, the damage will create a domino imbalance effect, which negatively impacts the performance of our Sensual Body, limiting our access to full sensual expression. We avoid the places we've hurt and become over-dependent on other parts. As a result, our Sensual Expression becomes more distorted until we are left moving through the world sensually crippled and not understanding why we feel disconnected and disembodied.

What does this look like? Let's go back to the person who was told, "Boys don't cry." Crying and showing vulnerability is the power of Peace. Peace is the Sensual Expression of love and acceptance. It is the nourishing softness that creates safety, trust, and connection. Peace just received injury through the messaging of "Boys don't cry. Suck it up, crybaby." If this goes unaddressed, the domino effect often leads to one of two outcomes. One, the person becomes a martyr or victim, unable to stand up for themselves and assert boundaries. Or, two, they build scar tissue and become inflexible in their Peace expression. Unfortunately, this is also called "being a man," being professional and keeping it together, aka, the building block for toxic masculinity.

The journey of Sensual Intelligence teaches us to have a conscious relationship with all 7Ps, so we have access to all of our expression and *choose* how we are in the world, rather than be pulled into reactionary states.

Like Riding a Bike

So how do the Sensual Body and the Sensual Expressions (the 7Ps) work together to form Sensual Intelligence? Let's compare the interplay of the Sensual Body (Embodiment, Self-love, Mindfulness, and Community) and the 7Ps (Pleasure, Play, Passion, Peace, Psyche, Philosophy, and Power) to a bicycle.

The Sensual Body is the essential components of a bike: the frame (Embodiment), gears and brakes (Self-Love), wheels (Mindfulness), and a place to ride (Community).

In order to ride a bike, you have to check:

Do you have all the parts for your bike?
What is the state of your bike parts?

Is your bike frame (embodied awareness) taken care of and steady? Or is the integrity compromised by invisible stress fractures?

Are your tires (mindfulness) pumped, or do you have a flat or possibly a slow leak?

Have you oiled your chain (self-love), or is it rusty and squeaking? How about your brakes? Do you overuse them?

Where are you bike-riding (community?). Are you on a country road or on the sidewalk?

The 7Ps of Sensual Expression are the individualizing details of the bike and its features; in other words, the type of bike you ride. Is it more of a mountain bike, a road bike, a hybrid, an electric, a tricycle, a fixie?

The level of relationship we have with each of the Sensual Body and 7Ps determines both how we experience the world and how the world experiences us.

Are you tending to your bike parts, and how are you tending them (Sensual Body).

What kind of bike do you have (7Ps and SQ Type)?

How are you riding it? Through what terrain? Are you riding safely and optimally for the type of bike and the environment in which you ride? Do you know how to fix your bike when it has a problem?

Everything in this book provides the lay of the land, so to speak, so you can become deeply intimate with your "bike" (yourself) as you ride through life.

The goal is to cultivate an active and conscious relationship with all parts of yourself—body, mind, heart, and community—so that you can take full advantage of your gifts and the world around you.

Sensual Intelligence is not about achieving "perfection." There's no "perfect" bike, just as there's no one perfect Sensual Intelligence. Therefore, it is up to us to know our bikes (ourselves) and how we ride them (live) in the world.

Chapter 7 Summary

- The Sensual Body and Sensual Expressions compose Sensual Intelligence.
- The Sensual Body is the building blocks of SQ: Embodiment, Self-Love, Mindfulness, and Community.
- The Sensual Expressions, the 7Ps, are how we express our Sensual Bodies, conduct, fuel, and motivate ourselves.
- There is no perfect or better SQ Expression than others; they each have their contributing gifts.

Chapter 8

THE SENSUAL INTELLIGENCE TYPES

"If we want to be healthy and fit, then we work out. Everyone has different skills, strengths, and flexibility. So some of us have stronger thighs while others have more flexible spines, and so on. The same goes for the sensual expression. The part of our sensual expression that is most dominant (the one that we use in the majority of our interactions) is our Sensual Intelligence Type. Check out www.Shawnrey.com/book-resources if you want to take the Sensual Intelligence Type Quiz."

The Sensual Intelligence Type is our go-to way of expressing our sensual bodies. It reflects who you learned to be to survive, as best you could, with the circumstances and resources you were given. It is influenced by exposure, accessibility, and available resources (including education and safe community). They include The Sensualist, The Creative, The Domme, The Intellect, The Mystic, The Diva, and The Empath.

Someone whose strength and ability is predominantly found in Pleasure, their Sensual Intelligence type will be the Sensualist. For the person with more dexterity and tendency in Peace, their sensual intelligence type is the Empath. A Sensualist and an Empath perceive and act distinctly from one another. However, no Sensual Intelligence Type is superior to the other. They are each perfect and skilled in their way.

THE SENSUALIST

The Sensualist is all about feeling good. Some may call them hedonists because they pay attention to their sensual nature. Bring on the scents, the furs, the candlelight. Or, for the modern Sensualist, they can lose themselves in the thumping bass of the music, the psychedelic lights, and magical enhancements. They were born for the pleasures of the flesh and appreciating the beauty of all things.

Their knowledge of the body is second to none. Sensualists know what they like, and if they don't, they aren't afraid to experiment and experience.

Origin:

Often, the Sensualist becomes a Sensualist because they are considered "beautiful" in their culture and have been treated with the beauty bias[5] or pretty privilege. They discovered Pleasure and the body's power early on, sometimes by their empowered discovery; sometimes, this is forced on them by abuse.

Power:

- Connection to the body, Pleasure and beauty
- Kinesthetic
- Attention to detail, especially what brings sensual enjoyment, bliss, and ecstasy
- Present in the moment
- Makes the most out of any situation because they savor the sensation of an experience

---

[5] Tomas Chamorro-Premuzic. "It's Time To Expose The Attractiveness Bias At Work." Forbes, 17, July 2019, https://www.forbes.com/sites/tomaspremuzic/2019/07/17/its-time-to-expose-the-attractiveness-bias-at-work/?sh=4127288f1324

Weakness:
- Indulgent, sometimes lazy
- Superficial and short-sighted
- Short-term, instant gratification

Secret Fear:
People only care about me and want me for my body. No one knows who I am; they only see the shell. Will anyone want me if I have physical blemishes, or if I am not always "turned on", or giving pleasure?

Secret Desire:
To be loved for more than their body. To be seen and treated with depth and respect, not just as temptation and a prize to be won.

Lesson:
Open up your heart and allow yourself and others to be perfect and acceptable just as you are. Don't let the pursuit of beauty and pleasure take over your life.

Recommendations:
- Learn more about the origins of the Sensualist in Chapter 17, Pleasure
- Learn more about Self-Acceptance and Self-Love in Chapters 12 and 23

THE CREATIVE

Ebullient and effervescent, the Creative has a way of bringing play, curiosity, and exploration everywhere they go. They can be funny and charming, but don't let their joy fool you into thinking they do not also have substance. The Creative is a visionary, and their humor comes from their unique world perspective.

If "Don't take life so seriously" was a person, it would be the Creative. They embody the inner child, connected to their imagination, creativity, a touch of magic, and a dash or two of mischievousness.

Origin:

The Creative chose to look cute to seem harmless and not a threat. They likely desired to be a certain way, but this desire could have been seen as a threat or veering away from their role's expectations. So they became almost chameleon-like and non-threatening. They can fit into many different situations because they did not put their foot down and make their presence known. They did not ground themselves in their power and desires.

Power:

- Clear connection to the inner child
- Able to access childlike wonder, playfulness, creativity, and keeping things lighthearted and those around them filled with cheer
- Diffusing a situation with whit, laughter, or sarcasm

Weakness:

- Feels like they are not taken seriously
- Doesn't have a sense of claiming what is theirs
- Not grounded
- Does not like to take responsibility because it feels burdensome and constricting

Secret Fear:

I'm afraid I won't be accepted when I show the real me. What if I show my true self and I'm judged, lacking, or not good enough?

Secret Desire:

To have their creativity and playfulness be taken seriously. To feel grounded in their body and intuition. To step into their power and be recognized as a force. To have others also play with them.

Lesson:

You are safe and wanted just as you are. You do not have to pretend to be anyone else, make anyone happy, or be entertaining.

Recommendations:

- Learn more about the origins of the Creative in Chapter 18, Play.
- Learn more about being grounded and present in Chapter 17 and 22.
- Learn to hone your intuition in Chapter 20.

THE DIVA

Divas are passion embodied. Fully engaged, intense, and wild, nothing turns them on like raw, unfiltered living. There's no half-assing around a Diva. So, bring on the realness, the full self-expression, and emotional connection. What's the point in pretending or playing small?

Origin:

Sometimes, this person had to make themselves big to be heard and seen by their family. When the outside world dismissed them, they made themselves known and heard so they would not disappear and be discounted.

Power:

- Full of life, movement, and vitality
- Vocally and physically expressive
- Unrepressed, non-conforming, catalyst
- Champions of change

Weakness:

- Can feel misunderstood or "too much"
- Reactive. Inappropriate outbursts.
- Emotions can get out of control and dramatic

Secret fear:

I will not be seen or loved as they are. No one will know how to hold or match my energy. No one will see how my heart wants to be soft and held. I will have to hold myself back and make myself smaller to be accepted.

Secret desire:

To be seen, held, and accepted, for all of who they are, both in their fire and their vulnerability.

Lesson:

Your passion is valuable and powerful. However, you are also soft and gentle, and your fire can be a Sempiira. You do not always have to push to be seen.

Recommendations:

- Learn more about the origins of the Diva in Chapter 19, Passion.
- Learn more about being held in Community in Chapters 14 and 15.
- Learn how to skillfully wield your fire in Chapters 13 and 21
- Finally, read Chapter 23 for softening

THE MYSTIC

The Mystic can also be called the Priest/Priestess. They are magical and wise, connecting to the mysteries of existence beyond the tangible. They traverse the depths of mind and spirit.

Origin:

The Mystic does not necessarily come from a religious background. Instead, they developed a spiritual and energetic view of the world. If something unwanted and violating occurred to their body, they felt that the body was wrong. They chose that there was something better and more advanced than the body. To be human and earthly also means to be dirty and vulnerable. Therefore, they would rather not deal with the body at all.

Power:

- Psychic, able to see 'behind the veil'
- Deep connection to spirit, God, magic, energy, ancestry
- Devoted, ceremonial
- Wisdom keepers and seekers

Weakness:
- Disconnected from the body.
- Can exclusively live in the spirit realm, therefore neglecting their body and "mundane" relationships
- Can be afraid of the body because they view it as a sin, low vibration, or un-trustworthy

Secret Fear:
If I come back to my body, I will be vulnerably human. Perhaps not special and perhaps ordinary.

Secret Desire:
To create a divine connection between Heaven and Earth. To feel safety and peace with body and spirit.

Lesson:
Your body is also your home. It is a sacred place worthy of your love and attention. Your body is a vehicle to the divine as well as divinity itself.

Recommendations:
- Learn more about the origins of the Mystic in Chapter 20, Psyche.
- Learn more about being in the body in Chapters 10, 11, 17

THE INTELLECT

Intellects experience the world primarily through their mind. Either more scientific and philosophically leaning, of thoughts, theories, analysis, imagining, questioning. The mind is a place where they roam freely and sometimes exclusively.

They love doing the research, checking up on all the facts. For the Intellect, learning and figuring things out is just as much of a turn-on as being knowledgeable.

Origin:
The Intellect shows up when someone has emotional drama in their upbringing, especially if their household did not have a sense of rational meaning-making and was purely emotionally driven. They seek to create safety out of sense-making facts and data.

Power:
- Observant and analytical
- Intrigued by research and finding things out
- Discerning and unbiased. Able to see things with a clear, balanced lens
- Able to create sense and order out of chaos and confusion

Weakness:
- Over-dependence on the brain and facts
- Misses or dismisses emotional cues from others
- Always in problem-solving mode
- Overthinks. Stuck in their head. The brain never rests

Secret Fear:

I will be exposed for not knowing what to do or how to explain my life or actions. I will be left alone and not understood.

Secret Desire:

To feel their heart, or want to feel their heart and connect with others in an emotional, heart-felt way, without feeling awkward or forced.

Lesson:

You cannot know everything. The way to the heart is through the unknown. Sometimes you have to embrace the mystery.

Recommendations:
- Learn to connect to your body in Chapters 10 and 11
- Open to softening your heart in Chapter 12
- Explore the unknown with Chapters 18 and 20

THE DOMINATRIX/DOMME

The Dominatrix/Domme can also be called the Achiever. Their characteristics are the definition of "success" in current society. Hence, a bit of arrogance comes with the territory. They love to be in charge of life—control, power, rules, and structure is their happy place. Sex and intimacy are often scheduled on their calendar, not spontaneous unless they planned it that way. They tend to be quite specific about what they want, when they want it, and how they want it, and expect it to be that way. They are not afraid to let you know if you fall short of their expectations.

The Domme is a powerhouse. But, they can also feel aloof, intimidating, and unapproachable. They rule from their head. Their presence fills the space with calm, commanding, magnetic energy.

Origin:

They learned what it means and what it takes to be ambitious, independent, and successful. The Domme learned to be the shining example and take care of their family. These Power types were very studious, and their behavior was rewarded by praise, recognition, money, and business opportunities.

Others did not have power over themselves and their situation as young people, so they made it a point never to need anyone again. Power, control, and mastery are their primary source of inspiration.

Powers:
- Take charge, leadership qualities
- Naturally strategic, ambitious, and driven.
- successful and savvy in their field and "have their shit together"

Weaknesses:
- Use their body only if it enhances performance, accomplishment, and dominion
- Controlling, domineering, and judgmental
- Difficulty softening for connection and intimacy, and letting others in. Closed off
- May not know who they truly are beyond accomplishments

Secret Fears:

I am not wanted beyond my accomplishments and what I can do for others. I will lose credibility and worth if I show fear, doubt, or vulnerability.

Secret Desire:

Freedom and genuine connection. They want to let go, let loose, and play. They want to feel their body. They want to be able to trust and let go.

Lesson:

You cannot always control the outcome. So, soften your grip on control, trust, and let others in. Vulnerability is powerful.

Recommendations:

- Learn more about the origins of the Domme/Dominatrix in Chapter 22, Power.
- Learn more about softening and opening in Chapters 23 and 18.

THE EMPATH

The Empath is open-hearted, nurturing, flowing, and a peacekeeper. They open their hearts and care to others, often at their own expense. This sensitive soul leads with their emotions and intuition. Empaths have characteristics usually attributed to feminine and maternal energies, though they are of all genders. Their ability to care and feel for others lends this quality.

Origin:

At some point in life, they were initiated into care-taking. The initiation could have been motherhood, caring for a parent, or resulting from a need to keep the peace in their surroundings. The Empath learned to control her environment by nurturing and being extra vigilant of their surroundings. They often do not realize this need for control because it is so soft and under the guise of nourishment. However, just like the womb creates a nourishing container, the Empath strives to create an environment that is also highly regulated and controlled to keep things safe.

Power:
- Nurturing, loving, caring
- Attunes to others' emotions, high emotional intelligence.
- Ability to de-escalate a situation and create harmony, flow, and connectedness

Weakness:
- Martyr and victim. Takes on everyone's problems
- Self-neglecting. Forgets about their own needs
- Overwhelmed and anxious
- Poor boundaries.
- Lack of feeling sexy, desirable, or desiring

Secret Fear:
Who am I without the container, without the control? Will I cease to be? Will I be safe? Who is going to hold me? Am I worthy of being taken care of as well?

Secret Desire:
Just on the other side of the yielding and softness is a fierce tsunami of need, desire, and want that could drown the earth. They need and want to be held as much as they hold others. They want to be both needed and set free. What they create for others is what they desire to make for themselves: a safe environment where they can be free and express themselves.

Lesson:

Learn to be centered yet open. Not only is it OK for you to take care of your needs first, it is also imperative that you set boundaries to support and delight in yourself.

Recommendations:

- Learn more about the origins of the Empath in Chapter 23, Peace
- Learn more about boundaries and standing up for yourself in Chapters 22 and 19
- Learn to delight in yourself in Chapters 10 and 17

Chapter 8 Summary

- The Sensual Intelligence Type is our go-to way of expressing our sensual bodies. It reflects who you learned to be to survive.
- The Sensual Intelligence Types are Sensualist, Creative, Diva, Mystic, Intellect, Dominatrix/Domme, and Empath.
- They each have their strengths, weaknesses, and lessons to help them navigate successfully and joyfully in the world.

Chapter 9

COMING OUT OF THE DARK

> Sweet Nectar
>
> *You open to me like a flower.*
> *Petals unfurled, a rosebud in bloom*
> *I am bee who sips of your nectar*
> *As your pleasure kisses my lips,*
> *Darkly and so sweet.*

Danielle, a Dominatrix SQ Type, is a 43-year-old lawyer who experiences her body as a vehicle that she is obligated to keep healthy for optimal performance. She eats a measured, health-conscious diet, and she runs every day. However, she doesn't feel sexually satisfied with her husband. At the beginning of their relationship, the sex was decent. It was never "amazing," but that hadn't mattered before because they both had similar life goals, were career-driven, and had a great friendship circle. Now she wants to have more sex. She admitted after further inquiry that she wants to feel passion for life overall, not just in her marriage. She reminisces about the Halloween party she and her husband attended where she "dressed like a slut," and felt wild and daring. She wishes she could be more like *that* Danielle every day, but she feels stuck.

Danielle followed what society told her was right and good. She trained herself to excel ideally in her career and create a life that, on the outside, was picture perfect. She has the job and a handsome, successful husband. Her calendar is full of plans with friends, and she always manages to check things off of her seemingly never-ending "To Do" list. At this point, she can go on autopilot and get through her days without feeling anything.

Without. Feeling. Anything.

If you, like Danielle, have felt numb, shut down, and trapped in your life, you are not alone. It is common to think that being numb or ignoring ourselves is safer than facing painful and uncomfortable truths and exposing our vulnerability. If you have longed for that sense of aliveness, joy, and pleasure but have felt blocked or afraid, take a deep breath. It's going to be OK. *You are going to be OK.*

You, like Danielle, probably have a secret yearning. It is a desire so deep it can be excruciating to dig up. The secret yearning for Danielle was to *connect with her body, open her heart, and calm her mind:* the journey of the Sensual Body. This hunger betrayed itself through the strain of Danielle's shoulders and the tightness of her jaw, and in the judgments she made about herself and her husband.

Put your attention on your body right now. You may notice a tightness in your belly or a slight holding of breath if Danielle's experience resonated with you.

The language of the body is a language that seems secret, but is the most intimate and telling of internal whispers. When you allow yourself to listen to the voice of your body's wisdom, you will understand the power of Sensual Intelligence. So, the first thing you have to come to terms with is that you *do* matter.

Danielle forgot that she mattered. She focused so much on her job, expectations, and doing the right thing that she overlooked *herself*. She stopped putting herself, her needs, desires, even her doubts, especially her doubts, into her life. Everything and everyone else had taken over. Danielle didn't know this yet, but she would soon learn that she does not feel sexually satisfied because she has disconnected from her body, closed her heart, and let her logical mind take the wheel. She is in a prison of her own design.

Leaving no room for softness, surrender, play, and joy is like stranding a sunflower in a dark cave and expecting it to live because you put dirt on it. You cannot overly compartmentalize your life and expect pleasure and fulfillment on demand. Perfectly controlled, disembodied schedules stifle sex, romance, and relationships. If you want to experience joy and pleasure in your relationships, your entire lifestyle has to support and validate joy and pleasure, not just on special occasions. Sensual Intelligence permeates our lives in all its facets. We are designed to have structure *and* be wild and free, play and explore, dig down into the depths of our beings, and soar to soul-expanding heights.

Danielle felt stuck because she inextricably linked her freedom of expression to her sexual expression, which is a trap most people fall into. We're taught to view a freely expressed body as automatically sexual, which is why the body is seen as deviant. I cringe at phrases like "dress like a slut" because it is a misguided and dangerous phrase for at least three reasons.

1. "Slut," though there have been movements to reclaim this word as an empowering term,[6] is still often used as a pejorative word to shame women who exercise their sexual sovereignty.

2. "Dress like a slut" assumes that someone, typically a woman, who dresses in certain clothing—in this case a short, form-fitting dress and a blue bob wig—desires sex.

3. Freely experiencing one's body in a way that pleases the senses is not automatically and exclusively sexual.[7]

---

[6] Janet W. Hardy, Dossie Eaton. *The Ethical Slut*, (New York: Ten Speed Press, 2017).

[7] For those interested in what Sensual Intelligence tools I used with Danielle, we first did a softening with Peace (Chapter 23). From that place of softness and surrender we explored Pleasure (Chapter 17). We couldn't go directly to Pleasure because her Power energy (SQ Type Domme) was too demanding and judgemental.

But I understood where Danielle was coming from. When she dressed in that costume, she accessed a sense of freedom, joy, aliveness, and power. She enjoyed the look and feel of her body in that outfit. And this is *sensual*, not sexual. Freedom of expression in your body does not automatically lead to anything sexual. It is an experience itself that many of us are robbed of because sensual intelligence has been lost.

Some people go to festivals or travel to foreign places to find this sense of freedom and joy within themselves. Festivals and exotic travel are great for some but not accessible to everyone, and it still may not quench the yearning when you're back at home, getting ready for work. Joyful, embodied fulfillment is a way of being, perceiving, and living in the world, and you take it everywhere because it lives inside of you. It *is* you.

Embodiment, Self-Love, Mindfulness, and Community are the Sensual Body because they are the foundational, everyday tools you need to access your Sensual Intelligence all the time, in every situation.

Yes, you can play at work. Yes, you can experience peace while parenting. Yes, you can show power through surrender during sex. In fact, you *must* learn to find and appreciate these moments to be fully present.

We are embarking upon a journey to liberate ourselves from societal expectations, mandates on who we are supposed to be, how we are supposed to occupy our bodies, what stories we can and cannot tell. Our pilgrimage is to discover and reclaim our birthright: the light hidden inside of us.

Every time I have taught a class, coached, or spoken on stage to introduce this journey, people always come up to me and say the same thing: "You gave me permission to feel myself in a way I have never felt before."

The following chapters show you how to tap into your Sensual Body: Embodiment, Self-Love, Mindfulness, and Community, so that you, too, can feel this permission.

Chapter 9 Summary

- Just because life may look good from the outside does not mean that it is the kind of life that gives us satisfaction.
- We can feel stuck and unsatisfied in our lives and relationships because we have done what we were supposed to do, rather than what is true to our human expression.
- When we connect to our Sensual Intelligence, we sojourn into the cave of wonders, discovering pieces ourselves.
- Each piece illuminates a different truth about ourselves, allowing us to see ourselves fully and start living in alignment.

Chapter 10

THE JOURNEY OF THE SENSES

> *We are always creating. Every encounter in our lives presents an opportunity to be even more fully present and embodied. We don't have to be the dancer whose soul leaps and spins, or the painter who ravishes the canvas with color and charcoal. We do not have to be the writer with her sibilant syllables that sensually slither, smoothing, soothing, and softening. We can be ourselves, creatively interacting with our world through our bodies, using our senses to beautifully craft life.*
>
> ~~ Excerpt from *The Sensual Artist's Prayer*

We are SENSE-ual beings. Period. Aside from a few exceptions, humans were designed to interact with, receive information, and express through our bodies and senses. Sensual Intelligence, at its most basic, is allowing yourself to sense. Get in touch with your senses. Have fun with your senses. Be artful with your senses.

Sense-You-All—sense *all* of yourself, and delve into the cave of wonders that is your Sensual Intelligence.

In this section, we will start to create a healthy, conscious relationship with the antenna of your body. Think of your senses as miniature satellites all over you, gathering information about yourself and your environment. Your senses can take you to incredible places if, and only if, you know how to use them.

The biggest crime to humanity is to possess a tool that can unlock Heaven on Earth and never use it. Intimately connecting with your senses gives you the creative, artful foundation for building your SQ. Don't let that tool go to waste!

We are the art. We are the artists. We are the painters, composers, dancers, authors, sculptors, and our bodies are the art. We start with a blank canvas, an empty score sheet, a bare stage, and then we create. Just as a dance and a painting are symbolic of life, showing us possibilities of living, sensual mastery is a way we can share and embody our imaginative selves.

Our art is a collaborative endeavor, where we allow ourselves to be moved by the spirit of the muse, to be a vessel of the divine. We open ourselves to be completely connected with the art of our life at every moment, constantly creative, ever engaged, and alive.

We are moved when we go to the ballet; we are touched and changed at the crooning of a poignant ballad. We are forever altered by artists who know their craft and offer it in its purest essence. We are such artists, invited to co-create the art of living, sensually intelligent, conscious, intentional, and aware. And these are our tools: Awareness, Acceptance, Appreciation, and Artful Application.

Awaken Awareness

Awareness opens the doors to perception and permits us to sense what is—without judgment. Awareness is an awakening to the truth of yourself and your experience. It is sacred, and it is vulnerable. It involves alternating between softening, allowing, and laser-sharp focus. Awareness is the opening and discovering of the Self. It is an inner truth that becomes known to you and will feel like you are waking up. It will invigorate and create a world of possibility.

Sometimes this gift comes from something positive that happens in life. It is direct, miraculous, and beautiful. One example for me was seeing my Aunt Carolyn laugh. I was always self-conscious about the color and crookedness of my teeth, so I kept myself small and didn't show my teeth when I smiled.

One hot, swampy, Louisiana summer, I sat with the grown folks as they traded stories. And then it happened: she laughed. She threw her head back, opened her mouth wide, and laughed from her soul. It was a wild and abandoned cackle that hit the air like a sonic blast! I was startled, dumbfounded, and at that moment, awareness awakened. I wanted to be like this woman, so free, full of joy, loud, and proud. Her exuberance was a contagious gift. It was permission to be myself. After that, I never held back a laugh again.

Other times, awakening awareness comes from something dark, and you have to dig deep to find yourself. These are times when it feels like reality has pressed down on us, and we are collapsing under the force. That happened when I was 16, and my mentor molested me. The awareness awakened the moment I stood up in front of the dance class and heard the first notes of the music. Something inside of me cracked open. I felt my power. I felt seen. I felt like myself again and knew that I would never let anyone take me away from myself again. Not like that.

Awareness is an embodied experience that moves and shifts your cells. You feel your body in a way that you never have and possibilities open.

SIP
Awaken Awareness

How do you awaken awareness? Ask yourself these questions:
- What do I notice, what do I feel?
- Where do I feel it in my body?
- What is the quality?
- What is coming up for me?

Always ask yourself these questions as they train your attention and the intimacy you have with yourself. We cannot change what we do not know and cannot sense.

Acceptance

Acceptance is looking at and being with a situation for what it is, without judging it to be 'good' or 'bad.' It is being present with what is real and true about, as opposed to the story you tell yourself about it. Acceptance does not imply that you roll over and let anything happen to you. Rather, it is opening yourself to the gift of being in the present moment, allowing it to unfold as is. Another way to describe acceptance is to release resistance. This is because acceptance is active and alive, inviting you to see yourself and the situation with fresh eyes and an open heart. It makes space to make choices from a grounded place of truth.

Again, going back to the experience that started it all, while I was doing the "Deliver Us" dance, in my mind, I was going through all of the times my mentor touched me, the pain and confusion I felt. My body moved, pressed, stretched, and danced every moment, allowing me to bring myself *right here. Right now.* I am Shawnrey, here and now. Yes, those things happened to me. Yes, it hurt, confused, and stripped me of my sense of self. Yes, that is a fact. But now I am here. Now I feel my body. Now I am creating my own experience of freedom. That dance was my embodied dance of acceptance.

Acceptance is not denying what happened, it is being with it, working with it, facing it, instead of shying away and trying to hide or pretend it is not there. This does not make it good or bad. It just is.

We will go into more detail with acceptance in Chapter 12, the Journey of Self-Love.

> ## SIP
> ### Create Acceptance
>
> How do you create acceptance? People often think that acceptance is a mind thing, but it starts with the body. Our bodies tense up and protect us from perceived threats. If you notice you are holding your breath or that your breath is speeding up, this is often an indication of non-acceptance.
>
> The easiest way to access acceptance is through the breath. Breathe in and when you exhale, relax the body. Notice different places in your body that are gripping. Is it your teeth? Your neck? Your stomach? Your brow?
>
> Breathe in again, and every time you breathe out, let go of the tightness in that part of your body.
>
> After you release as much tension as possible, sit with it—sit with yourself—and just be.
>
> Then you can go back and ask yourself the questions in Awakening Awareness to bring a deeper self-noticing.

Attend and Appreciate

The third tool the sensual artist uses is attending and appreciating. To attend is to put your full attention on something, to bring your presence and energy. Attending is a magnificent art that the digital age and social media have severely thwarted. Every time we scroll, swipe, and mindlessly click, we train ourselves out of connecting. We reduce ourselves to reactive automatons, disconnected from who we are and mindlessly giving our attention and money.

Sensual Intelligence invites us to develop true attending, the kind of attending that allows us to feel at home in our bodies. We retrain ourselves to release reaching outward to fix what is "broken," or satiate a hunger that is not even ours.

After we attend, then we amplify that attention with appreciation. Appreciation is the choice to step into the gift—the learning—rather than collapse into the story of disempowerment, judgment, or regret. Appreciation is the act of growing ever more whole, even more in your power and expansiveness.

> ## SIP
> ### Attend and Appreciate
>
> We must start with slowing down to stillness to attend and appreciate. This is a stillness of the mind. Stillness allows you to give your focused attention. Start with just looking at nature, say, a tree blowing in the wind. Set a timer on for five minutes and put your attention—your energy—toward the tree. Notice the beauty of its shape, color, movement, and stillness.
>
> Take a deep breath and feel your heart expand and deepen into an appreciation for this display of life, how the existence of this tree gives you clean air to breathe, how its roots keep the soil steady and healthy, how it gives your shade. The rustle of its leaves offers a sweet reprieve from the stressor of everyday bustle.
>
> Do this with a tree or with an issue that may be bothering you. Ask yourself, "How can I lean in and go deeper? What is the deeper message behind my immediate perception? What is the gift in disguise?"

Artful Application

Artful Application is where the rubber hits the road, where you go from the laboratory to real life. Self-discovery—unearthing the facets of SQ—is the foundation. SQ gives you the tools and artful knowledge you need to start living all parts of your life sensually and intelligently. Whether you're with your significant other or standing up for yourself at work, Artful Application is an invitation to live out loud and change the world through profound empowered presence and action.

SIP
Artful Application

Journal Activity

Answer these questions throughout the reading of this book:
- Where and how does this show up in other parts of my life?
- How do I want it to enhance my life?

After reading this book, refer back to these answers and see if your responses and yourself have changed.

The Sensual Meditation

Let's get to it! We don't have to wait for a stroke of insight to awaken awareness, accept and appreciate, and create Artful Application in our lives. It's best to do this deliberately; this way, we train ourselves to connect to our mind-body-heart and increase SQ.

Lucky for us, the first step is easy. *Eat!*

This is not just any old eating. This is *sensual* eating, a practice of Sensual Intelligence through sensual meditation that can apply to all of life. The sensual eating practice is one of the simplest ways to train SQ. You can use anything edible for this exercise, but for the sake of continuity, I will use a strawberry.

Remember, Sensual IQ is the artful knowledge of feeling and being in all of life, even the most mundane and practical—*especially* in the most ordinary and practical areas of life. These are the areas where we go on autopilot and disconnect. Sensual meditation through sensual eating is a practice that profoundly affects people.

As soon as we look at food, our bodies create the enzymes needed to digest it.

When we slow down eating, we awaken our awareness of the food, which results in us experiencing and accepting our bodies and our senses more fully. We open the aperture of our senses, and more life is available. When we sensually engage with our food through seeing, smelling, touching, hearing, and tasting it, we digest better and absorb more nutrients.

The following few pages are my gift to help you dive deeply into your senses, feel what is possible for your body, and know the gift you are. I encourage you to not just *read* this but to actually *embody* the practice. We are still in the process of embodiment, and this journey is crucial.

Every word in this section takes you through Awakening Awareness, Acceptance, Attending and Appreciating, and Artful Application through your interaction with the strawberry (or any other food that you choose). This is training your embodiment practice. If you can open your body and senses to what I am sharing here, you will transform your life.

Sight

Say this: **"I drink in vision with my eyes."**

Modern humans are heavily sight-dependent. If the lights go out, we're doomed, stubbing toes, crashing into things, unable to function in the mysterious and scary darkness. We look at things to recognize, cognize, and categorize, and ask, "Is it dangerous? Is it edible? Is it a tool I can use?" We've got to "see it to believe it." Of all the senses, sight has been the most co-opted and de-sensualized. We quite literally miss the beauty of life, the incredible light show, the wondrous cinema and artistry that unfolds before our very eyes.

To actually *see* beautiful art, we only need to take a moment to stop and *look*, to awaken our awareness, accept, attend, and appreciate.

See the Strawberry:

Look at your food, your fruit, your strawberry. Allow your eyes to gaze upon it. Notice the richness of the color as light shifts along the fruit's body: the garnet red that shines richly, the yellow-brown flecks of the seeds nestled tightly in a hundred tiny grooves, the crisp, verdant green of the frilly top. Take your time and let your eyes dance and delight in the unique structure, textures, patterns, light, darkness. Gaze upon the strawberry as if looking at it for the first time, as if looking at your lover. Let your eyes move along the curves, the edges, the indentions, the protrusions, the unique expression of this fruit. Let its beauty massage your eyes.

See Your Body:

Take a moment to look at your hand with the same open curiosity as you did with the piece of fruit. (This is especially powerful to do in the mirror and to look at a part of your body that you judge, hide, or do not like.) See the lines, crevices, undulating colors, shapes, and textures in your palm and along the ridges of your fingers. Watch the play of light upon each tiny follicle of hair, the geometric tessellation of your skin. Let your eyes linger over the scars, and make yourself blush with the wide-open acceptance, mayhap, desire you pour over these love-starved parts of your flesh.

When a mother looks at her child or a lover looks at their beloved, their eyes cannot get enough of the sight. They emblazon the subject of their adoration straight into their heart. Look at your hand and body with that kind of love, and drink deeply of the sight of yourself.

Sight looks beyond what is on the outside and sees deep into the soul essence of a person. True sight joyfully drinks in the beauty of each unique and perfect expression.

Where in your life can you bring more reverence of sight and appreciation of the innate beauty already present?

Say these words to yourself: "I intoxicate myself with the vision that I am: powerful, present, and aware. I see, and I am seen. I am whole and complete."

Touch

Say this: **"What I touch, I feel, and what I feel, I can heal."**

Touch is the most essential of our senses. We literally *need* touch to survive. If newborns are fed but kept in a sterile environment without touch, they will suffer brain damage and developmental disabilities.[8] Left long enough without touch, they will die. It is no accident that we have the phrases, "a healing touch" and "tender, loving care".[9] Touch is life.

The skin is a direct connection between the brain and the environment. Through touch, we link to others, and our life is affirmed by contact with other physical beings. We are truly an extension of each other. When we touch, we send electromagnetic pulses through the membranes of our flesh. Our neurons branch out similar to the interconnected tree-root system deep within the earth. Just as the tree roots draw nutrients and send information between trees, when we touch, our skin does the same. When an infant's mouth touches the mother's nipple, information about nutrients and antibodies the baby needs travels through the skin, and the mother's milk creates it. All of this through a simple, crucial touch.

A hug, an accidental brush of shoulders, a firm handshake, the caress of a hand against the cheek, the soft and gentle touch that bring tears of love to your eyes, the strong and tender embrace that radiates safety and

---

[8] Ardiel, Evan L, and Catharine H Rankin. "The importance of touch in development." *Paediatrics & child health* vol. 15,3 (2010): 153-6. doi:10.1093/pch/15.3.153

[9] Ashley Montagu. *Touching*. (New York: Harper & Row) 1986.

belonging—all of these things say to your body, "I see you. You exist. I exist. You are not alone. We are here together, and everything is okay."

Touch the Strawberry

Feel the weight of the fruit in your hands. Let your fingers trail along its edges—its smooth and bumpy contours. Rub it so delicately that it tickles your finger pads. Revel in the contrasting temperatures as the coolness of the fruit's flesh glides along the warmth of your flesh. Softly pinch it between your fingertips, feeling the pressure, the slight give. Perhaps wet drops of juice squirt between the crevices of your hand. Perhaps it is sticky, gently gluing your fingers closed.

Touch your Body

The heart and the hands are intricately connected. The palms of your hands are the same diameter as a healthy heart. Additionally, the heart and limbs are made of the same mesoderm origin, meaning that they develop at the same time when we are embryos. When your hands touch skin, your own or another's, you touch with the depth and breadth of your heart.

Your palms have the power to pulse adoration, celebration, inspiration along every inch of the body, with every brush, caress, cupping, and grasping grip. Your hands can consume the gift of skin touching skin.

Love through your hands because your hands are a direct link to your heart.

Touch your body as if you are caressing a most cherished lover or a most beloved child. Learn to feel the distinct nature of these different kinds of touch. Feel the love pouring through your own hands, filling yourself up with nourishment, grace, peace, and beautiful acceptance.

Touch yourself as you have always dreamed of being touched. Let soft caresses leave a trail of shivers down your entire body. Try a gentle slap, kiss, tap, or long sensuous stroke. Use your teeth to nibble the fleshy pad of your thumb or the delicious textured flesh at the crook of your arm. Take a large bite and feel the tug, the hard and slick bone of your teeth, the muscled wetness of your tongue, the press of your lips. Close your mouth, and feel the small bit of self-administered pain and sensation on your arm as you bite down just a little harder.

Pressure, pain, tension, temperature, texture, shape, weight, contours, and vibrations, with the right intention and awareness, can all be a call to awaken deep healing, pleasure, and transformation.

Important Note About Touch

Your body is a temple of joy, pleasure, and exploration.

Your body is the vessel through which you connect with the world and how the world connects with you.

Your body is worthy of being touched and explored.

Your deepest pleasures are worthy of being revealed to yourself and for yourself.

If you have lived on this planet, you have had things happen to your body without invitation—violations and neglect, experiences that robbed you of your autonomy, sovereignty, pleasure, and peace.

For some, it was getting hit, slapped, or grabbed. It was the cold, empty air, the absence of skin-to-skin tenderness for others. These are touch traumas to the body. These touch traumas can warp our relationship with the very thing we were given to possess and love: our bodies.

Take this time and touch yourself with love. Give yourself the many, multitudinous types of touch. This is your body, and you get to heal and soothe each and every part of you that someone else touched (or neglected to touch) out of harm, fear, rage, or sadness.

> Reclaim the touch that has been taken away from you and make it your own. Slap your own ass, because it feels good; let it be something that you initiate, that you desire, that you own fully and completely. Embrace that you are the catalyst to the tingling energy of your own body. Caress the skin of your face, tickle the flesh of your cheeks, and hold yourself tight. The freedom to explore your body, limits, and sensations is absolutely Yours.

Smell

Say this: **"I draw in the gift of breath, the gift of life."**

Smell is the most ancient of the senses for all of life. Even single-celled organisms can detect scent chemicals to inform them about the world. Scent is deep in the ocean, wafting in the air, mixed in the dark underbelly of the earth, emitting from our pores. Scent is everywhere. We can quite literally smell fear and disgust, our pets can smell cancer and our arousal—and so can we, if we cultivate a relationship with smell.

How do we do this? Just stop and smell the roses—or, in this case, your strawberry.

Smell the Strawberry

Bring the fruit close to your nose and breathe in deeply. The molecules of scent enter your nasal passageway and tickle their way down your nose, throat, and deep into your lungs. It fills your body with so much aroma that you taste it in the back of your throat. Memories emerge from the odor. The olfactory system is intricately connected to our limbic system, evoking emotions and memories. A fragrance can unlock entire worlds. Your body instantly teleports to the moment where the scent was most potent in your life. A memory, like the elusive brush of butterfly wings or the crushing strength of an ocean wave, wafts in the air. The air we breathe in and out every second of every day of our lives is resplendent with remembrances and stories dancing in the air, unwittingly taking us to other times and places.

Allow your curiosity to open as you draw in your breath deeply. The fruit is exhaling its scent—breathe it in.

Smell Your Body

When I was in high school, going through puberty, I had the misfortune of thinking I was the "stinky girl." This was especially apparent during big musical productions because I was shy and confused about my body. Dancing in a big group of hormonal teenagers was terrifying, as I was sure they were all disgusted by my scent. I was so embarrassed about my smell that I erroneously rubbed baking soda all over my genitals to "eliminate the odor" and sprayed myself with copious amounts of body spray.

I did not know that baking soda on a woman's sensitive genital area was the worst thing I could do. I threw my pH balance off dangerously and suffered even more smell and pain. I did not know that my scent was natural and healthy and that what I and all of these teenagers needed was to feel love and acceptance for our transforming bodies.

If you deeply inhale the scent of your skin, especially in the potent areas that emit the wild, primal smell of our humanity—our crotch and armpits—you awaken and imprint upon yourself. Smell is primal, raw, connected to the earth. Every human has a unique scent, just like a fingerprint. As we get to know the smells of our bodies, beyond the perfumes and deodorants, we learn to sense our health, emotions, and arousal.

Breathe in deeply the warm, spicy, floral, pungent smells, sharp and subtle, that glide from your body, through the air, into your body again, creating an energetic cycle of self-loving affirmation. Revel in the scent of your skin, warm with life. Let your breath touch and massage you on the inside of your body. Feel the delicious experience of life caressing the oxygen through your veins.

Taste

Say this: **"I taste the pleasures of the world."**

Taste is the dance of the tongue, cheeks, teeth, palette, and the air we breathe. Ninety percent of taste comes from smell. They are irrevocably linked, yet we cannot lump these incredible experiences together. Taste is an intricate play of touch and smell, where the ethereal meets the tangible, spirit meets flesh, breath meets matter, and they bend and fold, crash together and separate, and make love to create something entirely new.

We taste with the silken muscles and cushioned fat of our tongues. The tongue has thousands of taste buds that reach and stretch, sensing the health and safety of anything we put into our mouths. Too much in our mouths, and we smother the air, making the taste buds dull. Too little in our mouths, and we do not have enough to taste. Neither stuffing our faces in a fit of gluttony nor starving ourselves—the feast-or-famine see-saw—serves us well.

Taste the Strawberry

Start like a snake, letting your tongue sample the air around the fruit till it softly lands on this tangible, solid piece of nourishment. When we taste something, we are imbibing its essence, the experience of its soul, and bringing it into our bodies. Taste, for this reason, is very intimate. It is a gift and a surrender to that which we are tasting. We honor the surrender by savoring every millisecond of the experience.

Bring the fruit to your mouth and drag it over every dip and valley of your lips. Purse your lips and expose the moist inner lining where the saliva and wet bones of your teeth slip and nestle. Slide the fruit fluidly over this sensitive skin. Open your lips even more. Suck the fruit deeper into your mouth, and flick your tongue over it. Now use your teeth to pierce shallowly at first, then deeper, sweeter, deeper still, till you bite through the fruit's flesh and your teeth gently *clack* together.

Chew slowly. Feel the clenching and flexing muscles in your jaw, your temples, and the ever-shifting press and release as your teeth come together, grind, cut, and let go. Notice the shift in texture on your tongue as the fruit morphs from solid to more and more liquid.

Taste Your Body

Let your tongue be sensitive and open. Allow your taste buds to quiver in anticipation. Feel the saliva-soaked, heated tip of your tongue delicately sample the tender flesh of your finger, palm, forearm. Take your time and delight in the sensational dance of bitter, salty, sour, astringent, sweet, pungent, and umami. Experiment with breathing and exhaling through your nose as your tongue flicks over your skin. Open your mouth and draw in the flavored air molecules above your precious membrane. Let your lips descend, grasp, and suction your body while your tongue swirls languidly, kissing, imbibing. Slow down, take your time to sip, taste, nibble, bite, slurp, lick, swish—creating space to savor yourself.

Sound

Say this: **"I vibrate and feel vibrations."**

Everything vibrates and creates a frequency, announcing its unique presence. When we are in utero, not only are we submerged in the rhythmic sloshing of our mother's breathing and embryonic fluid, we can also hear things outside of the womb, vibrating our still-forming bodies.

One of my favorite things to do is go to sound baths and sound healings. You enter a room with Tibetan singing bowls, wind chimes, meditation bowls, rain sticks, and many other instruments. You lay down and let the sounds, which are tuned to healing frequencies, wash over your body. The intention is to bathe the entire body in harmonious vibrations and transport you to internal peace and bliss.

Hear (the vibrations of) the Strawberry

Take a bite into the fruit and listen closely, hear and feel the vibration of your teeth biting through the cell walls, hear how the sound shifts and changes as your saliva rushes into your mouth and mixes with the juice of the fruit. Listen to the slurp as your saliva lubricates your mouth—the tart and sweet making your body's juices run. Listen to the rhythm of your chewing and the resounding echo of your moans as you enjoy the symphony of wet mastication—teeth on tongue curling around the sweet flesh. Let your body vibrate and moan, dance, and enjoy the music you create.

Hear (the vibrations of) Your Body

When we speak, our voices can transport people. Hypnotists and ASMR practitioners have mastered the art of their voices, creating soothing tones that slow the heartbeat and take us to hidden parts of our consciousness. When we are in the throes of passion and delight, be it from food or sex or something else entirely, our vocal cords create moans, groans, and exclaim pleasure and delight. The opening and closing folds of the vocal cords are indistinguishable from the glistening pink flesh of the yoni, the pussy, the vagina.

Open your mouth wide, open your legs wide, and relax your sphincter. The tension we hold in our ass, hips, and genital area reflects the tension in the jaw and throat and influences the power of our voice.

Hum from the depths of your body, like the great bellows of old. Start with your lips pressed softly together. Follow the vibration's travel up and down your spine. Relax your jaw, widen your mouth in a series of yawns: "ahhhhh," "ohhhh," "ooooo," "eeeee." Pay attention to how these simple vowel sounds shape and vibrate your body.

What stories come up, what energies come to life, what memories surface? What pains are quieted and soothed?

Remember, the words that we speak to ourselves and each other: "I love you," "I believe in you," "You are special" vibrate both our bodies and the bodies of another. Your voice itself can be a sensual healing frequency. Breathy, soft, and strong. Whispers, clicks, scratches, scrapes, growls, howls, babbles, laughs, rustles, pops, crackles, the caress of your breath whispering down the spine—it can all be a healing sound.

I hope this sensual meditation tingles through your body.

I love leading this sensual meditation. I am not just reading the words—I am the vessel of crystalline transmission, the beautiful language of our bodies reflecting like a prism of possibility. Reading the participants' body language, sensing where they want to go deeper, where they need more space and time to explore, where there is resistance and hesitation. That is what I have access to as a highly tuned sensual being, whose job it is to enlighten others to the vast beauty and possibility of their aliveness while creating a container of safety. Without fail, I always have someone come to me the next day and say, "Shawnrey, I can't believe what happened last night! I went home, and I was still buzzing from that thing we did yesterday with the fruit, and ended up having the best sex in my entire life! And we never even talked about sex!"

I love to share the magic of this work, and I want as many people as possible to experience their joy and aliveness as often as they can. Sensual Intelligence is not limited to the bedroom. This way of being is available all the time, in every situation.

Chapter 10 Summary

- We are sensual artists, using the tools of our senses, sight, taste, touch, sound, and smell, to experience the world.
- To co-create the art of living, we first awaken awareness using the senses.
- Then we accept ourselves as we are.
- Next, we cultivate and appreciate our bodies.
- I took you on a sumptuous, sensual journey with a guided sensual eating meditation.

Chapter 11

EMBODIMENT – CONNECT WITH YOUR BODY

Body Awareness + Body Expression = Embodiment (embodied awareness)

Open

Open your body to feeling, being, loving, and growing.
Expand and contract.
Breathe deeply
The soft cold penetration of air as it slides over,
through, and under
The tiny hairs in your nose
And into the dark wonder of
You

Embodiment is the coherent, integrated awareness and expression of the body. It communicates the experience one has of the world, within and without.

Sensual Intelligence is an embodied intelligence. It is the richness and the fullness of life in all its technicolor splendor. It is not exclusively held in the body, but the body is essential. Our intelligent bodies receive, interpret, and transmit the wild dance of life through the bones, muscles, skin, and organs independently from and in conjunction with the brain.

Though embodiment is integral, we rarely listen to what the body communicates. We ignore our bodies, telling ourselves it's too hard, too much work, or we just don't know how to listen. The truth is that we don't want to hear what our bodies have to say. We've been taught to shun and negatively judge many experiences that the body wants and needs. We learn that specific ways of being are not good or not allowed. And after a while, it becomes our truth. As a result, we don't know how to express, develop, and properly integrate certain aspects of ourselves.

The practice of embodiment is necessarily vulnerable because coherence necessitates porosity, the ability to expose ourselves to the truth of ourselves in the face of the demands of the world. Embodiment asks us to look at and fully feel ourselves and say, "Yes, this too, my body, is good and OK, even though it may not fit the ideals of the world."

That takes courage.

Embodiment is the clear channel between mind, emotions (heart), and the physical form. While this may seem simple, it's challenging. You have to trust yourself, trust the world, and trust yourself in the world. We build this trust by having a conscious, healthy relationship with body awareness and expression.

Body Awareness

> Your Body Knows
>
> *You don't need all the things.*
> *It's all right here in your body*
> *Your body is both the medicine and the gift.*
> *Your awareness, and being with yourself, is both the healing and the celebration.*
> *The air flows through your body*
> *Both healing and opening you up to the revelation of yourself and connection to others*
> *You are more than enough.*
> *You are a wonder.*

If you have ever felt disillusioned by the pace of the world or your place in it, or found yourself going through the motions of what "they"[1] say will make you happy, give you love, success, or acceptance, you're not alone. Or maybe you're just trying to survive the day. In any case, this feeling of dis-ease, constriction, and not belonging is because we have not learned how to belong to ourselves.

It can feel so hard to be at home in our skin. Our society tells us that we are fundamentally flawed, that our natural state is inadequate, so we abandon ourselves again and again. We search for acceptance and belonging outside of ourselves. It has come to the point where it simply does not feel safe to be yourself, let alone explore anything new. If we pay attention, this shows up in the body; through the words we say, the habits we have, how we feel about ourselves and others, and our awareness and acceptance of others. Our bodies know, but *we* don't listen.

However, it's a rigged game because this social system has abandoned itself, turned away from the wisdom of nature, the earth's cycles, life and death, and the values of diversity.

As much as 93 percent of communication is nonverbal. Posture, gestures, pace, space, voice tone, and pitch, all of these factors play a much larger role in what we communicate than our words. We constantly scan and read even the most minute of communication and expression. For most people, this happens unconsciously, and often this information is not used accurately because the body, heart, and mind are not communicating clearly.

Embodied awareness is the chance to embrace the blood and sinew of your being and know that it is enough in all of its expressions.

You are enough.

How do we open to this body awareness? The first step is to do a body scan. We have to bring our attention to the body. See, feel, and familiarize ourselves with our bodies. I learned my body scan technique from Jon Kabat-Zinn's book, *Full Catastrophe Living*[10]. The body scan is a mindfulness technique where you put awareness on your body, scanning it as a whole and part by part.

SIP
Body Scan
Carve out 5–20 minutes for this practice.

Lay down on your back in a quiet place, where you will have few distractions. You can keep your eyes open or close them. Just make sure you do not fall asleep. Breathe naturally and let your body relax.

Put your attention on your whole body as it is being supported by the surface underneath you. Feel your breath as it goes through your body.

---

[10] Jon Kabat-Zin. *Full Catastrophe Living* (New York: Bantam Books, 2013).

> Then, starting at the top of your head, put your attention on the top of your head. Feel the muscles of the scalp. Notice the sensations in your scalp and head.
>
> If emotions or thoughts show up, acknowledge them, and keep breathing.
>
> Repeat this process going down your entire body.
>
> Put attention on your face, back of your head, neck, and so on, till you get to the tips of your toes.
>
> Breathe

The body scan is an invitation to just be in your body, for yourself, and to bring your non-judgmental awareness to yourself. Body awareness allows you to let go of the unrelenting influence of your emotions, judgments, and thoughts about yourself and your actions, and just breathe and be present with what is. Notice the bodily sensations that different thoughts and feelings elicit, and then let them go. In essence, doing body scans is like saying hello to your body and its expression, as if they are your neighbors. You're not trying to change, judge, or shame your neighbors (or yourself). You're just noticing them and greeting them.

When I facilitate embodiment practices of body awareness, I start with the body scan because this helps people slow down and give space to be with themselves. Then I guide a *heartfelt* awareness of the body which I explain in Chapter 12, Self-Love. Heartfelt attention brings the practice of Self-Love to their relationships to their bodies.

The body remembers. The body does not forget things we have pushed out of our conscious awareness. How we breathe, where we relax, what parts of us tense up in protectiveness are the body's communication. So often, we are trying to fix, change, ignore, or hide. Taking the time to bring awareness and attention to our bodies is the only way to open a pathway of internal peace and communication that we need for our embodied awareness.

If you are interested in a guided Sensual Intelligence body scan and awareness practice, please go to www.ShawnRey.com/book-resources/.

Body Expression

Body expression is playing with the instrument of your body. Your movements, sounds, breath cadence, pitch, tone, tension, relaxation, and speed are your embodied expressions of you. This is how we communicate about where we are in our relationship with ourselves and others. If this relationship is harmonious, we feel energized, clear, joyful. We feel nourished by our bodies and our relationships. However, when we are not congruent, we feel unease, confusion, fear, or stuck.

As children, we tend to be very harmonious in mind, body, and heart. When we like something or do not like it, we do not try to hide, judge, or rationalize why we should or should not. We just do it. If we like chocolate cake, our minds say, "I like it," our little hearts flutter with joy and anticipation, our bodies express unfiltered delight, and we dance, sing, play with the chocolate cake. We enjoy every bit with no guilt, no shame, no stories, no excuses, no filters.

Then things happen in life that throws off our internal compass. The rules for how things should be, the messages of "look before you leap," "what will the neighbors think," "that's not what good boys or girls do,"—the unchecked hurt and power struggle of abusive households. We end up disconnecting from the innate wisdom of the body.

For example, look at how a child eats. When left to their own, they will take a million years to eat a cookie because they are so in tune with the sensuality of the experience. Eating is for escaping and numbing; rather, it is for delighting and enjoying.

One activity that I like to use in workshops I call the "Expression Challenge." I have participants pair off and face each other. Then I have them say the following words to their partner: "Thank you for expressing all of yourself. It is an honor to see, feel, and experience all of you. Bring it on!"

Person A is going to follow the body expression prompts I give. Person B represents all of life's obstacles, internal judgments, fears, and anything that could stop Person A from fully expressing. The challenge is for Person A to make their way from one side of the room to the other in the body expression prompt. Person B's job is to physically block them from getting to the other side.

What happens is a hilarious and raucous affair that creates an embodied experience of what we go through every day.

Often the prompts I use come from an earlier discussion with the participants on body awareness. First, I ask them to share what they are most afraid to have others see, what makes them uncomfortable, or where they hide. From there, I give them prompts like, "Unleash your inner diva and sashay across the room," "throw a temper tantrum," or "own the room like you are the CEO."

Everyone has varying degrees of expression, repression/suppression/denial, over-expression (exaggerated) of themselves. Some are shy folks who do not show themselves because they do not feel worthy, are scared of judgment, or taking up too much space. Then there are the folks who realize they've been *performing* themselves and not *being* who they truthfully are.

The point is to give everyone space to explore their body expression in a safe, fun, and supportive environment to have the felt experience of being with that expression. It trains the body and the mind in body awareness and body expression. We are not just stuck in our heads talking about our essential selves. We practice giving ourselves permission to embody and love all of ourselves and our expression. We stop hiding.

Your body deserves to be seen and heard. You get to be yourself.

SIP
Embodiment Cocktail Recipe

If you look at Sensual Intelligence and embodiment from a neuroscience perspective, you will see that every sensual, embodied experience comes with a particular blend of hormones and neuronal firing. Increasing embodied awareness and SQ gives you the ability to use the body's gifts consciously. I've listed the hormones, the feelings they elicit, and what embodiment activity triggers that experience.

But first, tune into your body and ask yourself: "What does my body need? What does my body want, deep down?

Then, try making a tasty "Embodiment Cocktail" using the ingredients below.

Dopamine: Feel Good Juice

Listen to music that thrills you, especially if it gives you the chills. Let the music stimulate your memory and marinate in your body.

Serotonin: Feel Happy Juice

Dance to the music that excites you, or play and be silly! The sillier, the better. It's not about doing it right; it's about doing it, period. Take yourself out of your mind and into the intelligence of your body.

Oxytocin: Feel Loved Juice

Get hugs and massages. Do not waste your time with fake hugs where you barely touch. Get in there and hug it out for at least 20 seconds, which is long it takes for oxytocin to activate.

Testosterone: Feel Powerful Juice

Get in a good, competitive, physical game. Good on you if you are growling, beating your chest, and ready to dominate something! Again make sure you are having fun. This is about giving your body experiential, embodied nourishment.

Estrogen: Feel Sexy Juice

Take a hot bath, melt into something sensual, or get down with strawberries. Revisit Chapter 10, Journey of the Senses.

> If you feel resistance, take a moment, be still, and breathe deeply. Slow, deliberate breaths allow you to slow down. Deep, slow breathing shuts off the brain's flight-flight-freeze-fawn response and turns on the parasympathetic nervous system, allowing us to relax and feel present.
>
> No matter what, start small and build your capacity. Be gentle, have fun, and take it one step at a time!

Embodiment and Imposter Syndrome

In her TED Talk and book, *Presence*, Amy Cuddy says, "Don't fake it till you make it. Fake it till you become it."[11] However, we don't have to 'fake' anything. We already *are* it. We do not have to fake what we already are. The "it," whether it is confidence, power, joy, whatever makes you feel like your best self, is not something that you have to conjure or create. The "it" is your birthright that has been buried under the confines of conditioning.

I'm asking you not to fake it because faking does not cultivate embodied awareness. I'm asking you, Sensual Intelligence is asking you to find and reclaim your "it" by creating unity of body, heart, and mind.

Penelope was in her mid-20s, a young Asian woman working as a data analyst in the tech field. Penelope's SQ Type is the Empath with an Intellect secondary. She was small-statured, soft-voiced, sweet, and accommodating. But, when she was relaxed, a mischievous little laugh would sneak into her words, hinting at a little bit of sass.

However, her laugh was rare because for a lot of her life, especially at work, Penelope felt like an imposter. Though she worked at a company she enjoyed, she was not in her desired department. She knew deep down that she was a strategist, but she had gotten filed in and stuck as a data analyst. At meetings, no one heard her soft voice, and every time she had an idea, someone else

---

[11] Amy Cuddy. Presence: *Bringing Your Boldest Self to Your Biggest Challenges*. (New York: Little, Brown Spark 2015), 295.

said it louder and then got the credit. She felt ignored, unappreciated, underutilized, and invisible.

To make things worse, the same thing was happening in her relationship. She and her boyfriend had been together for three years, and they still didn't live together, even though that's what she desired. When they visited his parents' home, her boyfriend wouldn't stand up for her when his mother spoke poorly of her, as if she wasn't even there. She felt like he didn't treat her as if she mattered. Penelope felt that she was being shut out of her own life, and she wanted the confidence to finally stand up for herself and get what she deserved.

When Penelope shared this, her voice was tight and strained. Her shoulders slumped forward, and she crossed her arms over her chest and belly and leaned her chin onto her hands. Her posture turned inward and slightly collapsed. Her body language projected defeat and insignificance while her words demanded respect. Her body and mind were at odds.

Imposter syndrome happens when our conscious mind communicates, "I deserve respect; give me the job," but we subconsciously embody, "I am small, I don't get what I want, and people do not listen to me." The result is incongruence and disconnection. Incongruence can look one of several ways, but the result is the same: it creates confusion. This manifests as a sense of dis-ease, i.e., imposter syndrome, anxiety, physical illness, and burnout. This disconnection is widespread because we have not had embodied awareness modeled. We live in a world of "do as I say, not as I do." We are told to "think before we act," which frankly means "do what society, propriety, and authority says to do."

I took Penelope through embodiment exercises to first help her gain body awareness to notice her body's communication to herself in various situations. As an unbalanced Empath SQ Type, she did not have firm boundaries, which is why everyone was "walking all over" her. However, because her secondary SQ Type was the Intellect, I knew that she would have the ability to study herself and take in information once she was made aware.

My approach with her was twofold: first, tap into her Intellect to share the information. Second, introduce her to embodying Power (Chapter 22) and Passion (Chapter 19).

I asked, "When you spoke about your job or your boyfriend, what did you notice happening in your body? Where did you notice tension, stuckness, burning, holding her breath, etc.?"

She became aware of her chest collapsing inward when she felt disappointed or even anticipated feeling disappointed. After establishing body awareness, Penelope then learned how to listen to and leverage her body's expression consciously so that she always had a choice rather than defaulting to reactivity.

I invite you to do this as well. If something resonates, use these teachings for your situation!

If the body communication is *not* embodied, it creates a sense of discord and confusion that people have to sort through and interpret. When communication is embodied, it feels trustable to everyone.

After six months, she changed her job position to one that brought her fulfillment. She spoke up for herself in meetings and rocked her performance review. That mischievous little laugh that was hiding before came out much more often, and Penelope found her confident, natural sass. It was buried underneath the expectations she carried and the "nice girl" she strove to be— the "nice girl" society wanted her to be. She transformed her negative mind chatter and body language into thoughts and embodied actions that supported her desires.

Now, when she talks about her boyfriend standing up to his mom (telling her to mind her own business!) and how they are decorating their new home together, she does it from an integrated place. She embodies her Sensual Intelligence in her unique way. It is not forced or prescribed. Her body already contained the blueprint for the life she wanted to embody. All she had to do was go on the adventure of finding and claiming herself.

Dropping into our Sensual intelligence allows us to embody and embrace our own perfection.

Come home into your body, come into your power, using movement, sound, and rewrite the stories of who you are.

> *"Thank you for being so supportive through my journey of finding and remaking myself. One doesn't get to be reborn as the phoenix without going through the ash phase." ~Penelope*

Why Art?

> The Muse
>
> *The muse has heard your pleas. She is here to inspire rapture, to take you on journeys unbound by convention and rules. She invites you to surrender to the purity of truth, nature, beauty, and your innate connection to the creative process.*

Your life is your greatest masterpiece.

Art, dance, and creative expression are the best ways to explore Sensual Intelligence. Art is the embodiment of freedom. We get to create ourselves as we are truly meant to be because there is no need for convention or inhibition. Art provides a laboratory to explore the unknown.

We love going to concerts because we allow ourselves unbridled, ecstatic expression. When we dance at a show, we express ourselves, heightened in our hearts and emotions.

Sensual Intelligence teaching combines the power of art, intuition, and heart connection, allowing us to access the parts of our minds that have not been co-opted, so we can experience the world in a new light.

I used to lead a program called Wake, Shake, and Elevate, a 15-minute dance party where people all over the world elevate their day by dancing together. It was fun because people brought their children, making us an international, intergenerational community of dancing, smiling, laughing, intention-setting dancers. The children experienced their parents taking care of themselves and being embodied. The adults got to hear the wise voices of the children's insights and intentions. We synchronized our breath and heartbeats through the dance and strengthened our connection with our bodies and each other.

Art can be a transformative experience. Through the proper guidance, embodied art can help you can take the inner, most sensitive parts of you and set them free, releasing pent-up emotions and worn-out stories that have been shaping you.

I lead people through the art that needs to emerge from their bodies. I help them birth the movements that are begging to be danced. Sometimes, it is a primordial reconnection to the body found through drumming on their own flesh, the kitchen table, or a wood and animal-skin instrument. The rhythmic thumping reconnects them to the earth and the beat of their body. Embodying art reminds them that *they* are a living drum through their heartbeat. They are art.

But beware, there is a way to do art (dance, poetry, and drumming included) that is disembodied. When you take an art form and distance it from Sensual Intelligence, it becomes disembodied, dry, and harmful to the psyche. I have multiple clients who were dancers from a young age, and they lost, or never experienced, the joy and freedom of moving their bodies and exploring self-expression. Instead, the art was a product, practiced for perfect execution rather than creative exploration.

One evening I heard the call of music, but I was tired after a long day of writing and being isolated. All I wanted to do was *walk* the stress from my body, not dance. Besides, my skirt was too short and my sweater too thick.

It is easy to lose ourselves in fear, division, uncertainty, and the monotony of just getting through the day. But art does not make logical sense—it makes spiritual, heart sense, and when the muse calls to you, you answer the call. She called to me through the music, and I found myself sweating, laughing, swaying, and shimmying in the summer sunset for almost two hours.

Sweat and joy soaked my sweater and short skirt, and it was good. It was medicinal.

Art is an invitation to come back to your body and celebrate the blessings you have. Use your smile, body, and spirit to spread joy wherever you can. Talk to your body with your art. Let the drum of your heart lull you in to your pleasure. Dance your life! Your embodied joy gives hope and permission to create a beautiful world.

Chapter 11 Summary

- Embodiment is body awareness plus our body expression.
- Embodied awareness is the coherent, integrated awareness and expression of the body. It communicates the experience one has of the world, within and without.
- Embodiment allows us to integrate, comprehend, and utilize our bodies' intelligence to enhance the fullness of our lives. It is the sense of feeling at home within yourself.
- The journey of finding the lost intelligence is an artful journey, with many twists and turns, just like poetry and dance.

Chapter 12

SELF-LOVE – OPEN YOUR HEART

Self-Intimacy + Self-Acceptance + Self-Integration = Self-Love

---

The Path of Love

Self-love is a journey of unlearning
So you can explore and discover the truth of who you really are, and want to be
Unbind from rules, and unclaim all the stories that are not yours
Un-embody the postures you were told would keep you safe
Un-condition and discover the sweetness of your liberation
Your reclamation,
Your pleasure,
Your power.

The Self-Love Journey

You are made from love. You are the extraordinary movement of over 100 million sperm cells, all dashing toward the incredible stillness of one egg. When the egg allowed the sperm to enter, they merged to create something new and magnificent: You. You are an eternal blossom, an act of self-love multiplied billions of times over. You are motion and peace, chaos and tranquility conceived in the darkness of the womb to be a light in the world.

Self-love is when you realize the exquisite work of art that you are.

Self-love is the act of seeing and accepting all parts of yourself. When you love and accept all of yourself, it is a joy to be in your body and mind. It feels good to share life, love, passion, and pleasure. Your pure essence shines through, and you are seen, chosen, and celebrated for who you are.

However, we are taught to feel at odds with our natural state. Many of us are in a non-stop cycle of fixing, changing, bettering, nipping, tucking, tweezing, plucking, shaving, losing, and bulking. And we hold back and hide the parts of ourselves we cannot change under acceptable masks. So we get stuck twisting, shaping, and manipulating our beautiful, weird, and magnificent selves to fit in the molds carved out for us.

When we try to fit ourselves into prescribed ways of being, the outcome is stress, depression, self-doubt, and anxiety. As a result, we can feel uninspired and disconnected from our bodies, clarity, greater purpose, while obligation dominates our very existence.

Sound familiar? This is the macabre soundtrack of adulting. This mind-numbing drone slowly tears us apart. It is painful. It is exhausting. It costs us our lives—and markets profit from our existential crisis by selling us distractions.

So what do you do? What do we do when our culture tells women not to express anger, rage, and other emotions that are not "nurturing"? What do we do when men are told not to express sadness, fear, or tenderness? What do we do when strict gender roles limit how our beautifully diverse bodies and minds exist and express in the world?

We have inherited a legacy of pain, imbalance, shame, embarrassment, policing, punishing, guarding, and forcing—so how do you break free?

What do you do?

Accept yourself.

Honor what is. Honor who you are now.

"What!?" you might be saying. "I can't just 'accept myself!' Who I am now isn't good enough. That's lazy! I won't succeed. I'll get stuck with… *this.*"

We are inundated with the message that there is something wrong with us and that to be more useful, we need to change who we are. We're told that who we are *now* is the problem, and the solution is who we can make ourselves be in the future.

Deep down, we're wondering:

Am I enough?

Is there something wrong with me?

Can I live in my own skin and love myself, be myself, trust myself, and still be accepted?

Can I be loved for who I am?

We grow by first being OK with exactly who we are, in all of our perfect imperfection—seeing our beauty, ugliness, truth and lies, mistakes and shortcomings, and aces and accomplishments.

This is an invitation to see yourself. Accept yourself. Celebrate yourself. Embrace the injuries, the blemishes, and the scars. And yes, even embrace the aspects that are considered exceptional or beautiful because even beauty and desirability can leave deep scars of not belonging.

How?

Practice unconditional Self-Love.

Self-Love Deferred

> *When I don't hold myself hostage, my creativity flows.*
>
> *I lay down in my bed, beating myself up, trying to make myself be productive. I was berating and belittling myself for not doing more, for not fulfilling my responsibilities. All this mind trash clutters my brain, and still, I wouldn't make myself—couldn't force myself—to write the emails, make the schedules, do the social media posts, stop obsessing about the things I don't have that I desire.*
>
> *I couldn't even force myself to meditate. Ha! I entered my "meditation" with an internal threat: "Focus and calm your mind, and get yourself out of this funk, or else!"*
>
> *Yeah. That shit doesn't work.*
>
> *Finally, I said, fuck it. And got up to take a bath.*
>
> *I chose, at that moment, to honor my body, my rhythm, my need to be gentle.*
>
> *And as soon as I turned on the knob for the water, something released inside of me, and I was suddenly very inspired to do all the things I was resisting. I didn't even take the bath!*
>
> *I listened.*
>
> *That was all that was needed: my body needed to be heard and valued.*
>
> *This reminds me, yet again, of my own teaching, of things I have learned years ago and have taught to others... Honor what IS first.*

Please do me a favor and fill out this sentence.

"I will _____ when I _____."

OK, now let's go deeper, to the heart of this exercise. We don't want sentences like "I will graduate when I have enough credits" or "I will pay off my house when I get out of debt."

We're looking for the next layer of depth in your sentences, the ones that have an element of judgment in them. Do you know what I'm talking about? I'll help you out. Complete the following sentences, and go with what pulls your heart.

I will feel confident when I _____.
I will love myself when I _____.
I will be OK when _____.

Keep going! Do as many as you can in 2 minutes.

OK, we're going to dig a little deeper. Maybe you actually wanted to write something like this:

I will feel peace when [*person, place, thing, situation*] does [*x action*].

For example, "I will feel peace when my girlfriend respects me."

Set your timer for 2 minutes and write down these phrases too:

I will _____ when [*person, place, thing, situation*] does [*x action*].

Great. Now, for some important news.

This sentence, "I will _____ when _____." is one of the most dangerous combinations of words in the English language. Why? Because you name the conditions you must meet to love, accept, and express yourself.

You may have sentences like these:

I will love myself when I get the job and succeed.
I will like my body when I lose weight.
I will know I am acceptable when I stop being depressed.

Or these:

I will have love and respect when society changes.
I will forgive my parents when they see the error of their ways.
I will be happy when someone gives me attention.

And so on.

Let's do surgery on this phrase.

Go ahead and get your mental scissors out, and hold that phrase out in front of you where you can see it clearly.

Now cut off all of that phrase except for "I."

Now place what you put after the word "will" after "I."

If your sentence said: "I will relax when I finish cleaning the house."

It should now say: "I relax."

If your sentence said: "I will get into a relationship when I have gotten my career off the ground."

It should now say: "I get into a relationship."

If your sentence said: I will have love and respect when society changes." It should now say: "I have love and respect."

What was the point of this exercise? It was to show you just how sneaky and pervasive self-judgment is. We say things like this to ourselves all the time, adding to the never-ending list of tasks we must do before we are good enough. We never think to question the origin and validity of this line of reasoning or ask ourselves, "Why can't I feel good enough and happy as I am now?"

The truth is, how we talk to and think about what we deserve shapes our lives. We want to be seen and accepted, even though we judge and hide what we cannot accept within ourselves. We live a love-deferred lifestyle, constantly starving ourselves of the self-acceptance we need to feel ease and worthiness.

Even when we point the blame at someone or something else, we still are keeping ourselves from love. It's not the person, place, thing, or situation out there that keeps us from feeling whole; it is ourselves.

Again, we do not live in vacuums. We are communal creatures, and we absolutely need love, touch, acceptance from others. Self-love is not a substitute for our human need to belong; Self-Love is the necessary companion, the other side of the equation, if you will, for creating sustainable and regenerative love and belonging for self *and* community. We need *both* to survive and thrive.

There is no escaping that there will be people who do not accept you. There will be people who do not honor and cherish the gift that you are. We operate within systems of oppression that disenfranchise vulnerable people. *All* of this is happening all of the time. But we have to start somewhere if we are going to create change.

Systems need to change, and the system can't change if societies don't change. Societies can't change if communities don't change. Communities can't change if families don't change. Families can't change if individuals don't change.

Any part of ourselves and our history that we cannot integrate comes out against others in "-isms," intolerance, and fear. Self-Love and pleasure protect us from the intolerance of others, and most importantly, protect us from *ourselves*.

Self-Love is a journey of weaving love and forgiveness with the pain and shame and honoring our bodies, which hold the stories of our lives.

Learning to love your body, ability, skin color, smell, sensuality, and pleasure is a sacred practice, a revolutionary and transformational act. It heals the wounds that so many of us carry that tell us that we are not worthy of our birthright of love, pleasure, belonging.

Self-love is the spaciousness that we give our growing, changing, learning selves to accept who we are, so we can become who we are meant to be.

Shameless Self-Love

In the Shadows

I've seen it. I've seen the other side of myself,
Of my darkness.
Of those parts I have put in the shadows.
Those parts that I hide to keep me safe,
To keep others safe.

I have found and looked into these places
Of hiding and gauding
And suppressing
And have felt their dark hunger
Tearing down our psyche,
Poisoning our lineages
And souring our hearts.
For what?
To be accepted into something that I did not make?
That I did not choose?
That did not choose me?

Tonight we unwind.
We unwind from the constraints that we thought kept us safe,
But have really kept us hostage.
We unwind, but we do not forget.
We unwind so what we do not suffocate,
So there is space to breathe,
To dance,
To dance,
To dance with the things we have kept in the shadows.

When I danced to this poem, it made me cry. You can find it on my Instagram account @shawnreynotto. Or just go to http://www.Shawnrey.com/book-resources for this information and more.

This poem honors our greatest teachers: our shame and shadows, the parts of ourselves that we want to hide. Shame has the power to keep us from enjoying and fully embodying ourselves because it says there are parts of us worth rejecting. But shame is also the compass for our healing because if we learn to embrace what we reject in ourselves, we discover how to be whole.

Brené Brown is a top researcher on authenticity, vulnerability, and living courageously. She came to fame after a TED talk about shame and has written multiple books based on her research, interviews, and her own life. She says, "Shame is the intensely painful feeling or experience of believing that we are flawed and therefore unworthy of love and belonging."[12]

Shame is internalized oppression. It is a learned survival mechanism for living and functioning in a society that rejected itself. It is meant to keep us in line, doing the "right thing," keeping with the status quo no matter the consequences to ourselves, as long as it is the socially correct thing to do. Want to control people? Don't do it with outside force—have them do it to themselves, from within. Fear of being ostracized, ridiculed, unwanted, and unloved are very real threats to our fundamental human needs of belonging and acceptance.

That nasty voice in your head that tells you everything you're doing wrong is shame. Especially around sex or sensuality, we tend to internalize a dichotomy of good and bad, with nothing in between.

Shame makes us preemptively reject ourselves before society can point out our flaws and shortcomings. It is the silent killer that eats away at us from the inside, feeding on our fears. Shame distorts our view of ourselves and shapes how we think, feel, act, and see the world and our place in it. As a result, we will twist ourselves into unrecognizable positions to avoid associating with the source of our shame.

---

[12] Brene Brown, *The Gifts of Imperfection* (Hazelden Publishing: Center City, Minnesota, 2010), 38.

In both my personal life and professional I have encountered many faces of shame. And healing shame is one of the most humbling and beautiful experiences I have ever felt or witnessed. You shed a worn-out and tired mold of yourself and reveal a blazing, strong, and pure heart.

How do you heal from shame? Love yourself back to wholeness.

A Shame Journey

I got genital herpes four days after my 28th birthday. I was utterly devastated. In my mind, I went from being a highly desirable, on-her-way-to-good-things woman to becoming the lowest creature to walk the earth. I felt dirty, unwanted, nasty, and every other rotten thing you could think of.

I felt shame because I believed a good, upstanding citizen would never have allowed herself to have sex before marriage. A *good* person wouldn't have herpes. If you have a sexually transmitted infection, you are dirty, unclean, and unwanted, especially as a woman.

Shame devoured me: my life, my self-love, my confidence, my self-worth. Shame told me that no one would ever love or want me. Shame told me I was so dirty that I should stop teaching. Shame told me I should not touch or be touched. Shame said that if I were a better person, I would not be in this situation and that this was proof that I was worthless and unlovable.

It doesn't matter what the origin of your shame is. It doesn't matter if it "makes sense" or not. It doesn't even matter if you think it's doing you good to keep certain parts of yourself bottled up and hidden because shame is like aggressive cancer. It starts in one area of life but spreads if left unchecked. No matter the source of your shame, it always has the same message. "I am a bad person. I am unworthy. I need to hide. I don't deserve to be treated well. What if anyone finds out? I should be punished." These thoughts warp your perception, actions, and relationship with yourself, making sure you never forget what you have done. Shame keeps itself alive by retelling the same loop of negative stories repeatedly, breaking you down.

What can we do? How do we release the grip of shame and trauma in our bodies, psyches, and lineages? How do we escape the dark shadow of shame?

I'll give you a hint: you can't do it with your brain. The process of healing is the same, no matter the circumstance. Shame is just the compass, pointing to aspects of ourselves we rejected long before the event that catalyzed the shame. Shame shows us what parts of ourselves we need to face, lean into, embrace, and integrate into wholeness.

The only way to truly heal shame is through the heart, through self-love. Self-love is the combined forces of Self-Intimacy, Self-Acceptance, and Self-Integration.

> *"This is healing from the trauma of being a woman in this sexist society. Embodiment practices for a broken-hearted millennial woman."*
> *~Andrea*

Self-Intimacy: Face it and Lean in

Self-Intimacy is being able to face yourself and lean in.

Whenever I share about having herpes, many women come up and whisper, "Thank you. I have it too. I've never told this to anyone before." People tell me that they gave up on love and dating because they could not face the shame of rejection. Instead, they preemptively reject themselves.

Shame is like a hot stove: we touch it and jump away. We avoid looking at it, at ourselves directly, because it reminds us of all the bad things. We'd rather avoid it and pretend it's not there.

The problem is that shame is internally divisive and flourishes in the shadows. So, as long as we're not facing it and shining the light of truth and awareness on it, it will continue to fester.

To face it and lean in simply means stating the facts; no more, no less. Shine the light so that it can no longer hide in the shadows.

Try this out now. You know exactly where to look. It's that place that makes your heart squeeze tight and pound in your throat. It's where you stop breathing and pretend that "everything is fine."

Take a deep breath. Put your hand on your heart. It's going to be OK. Look at that part of yourself, that place in your life, and just sit, breathe, and be.

Just sit with that seeing, be with it. See how it wants to run away and hide. Notice how it squirms uncomfortably at your witnessing.

When you are ready, you can say out loud: "I see you. I see you."

Self-Acceptance: Embrace Yourself

In Chapter 9, I described acceptance as the ability to look at and be with a situation for what it is, without judging it to be 'good' or 'bad.' Self-Acceptance is simply applying this spaciousness to yourself.

Think of the last loving hug you received or gave (or, if you have not received one, think of times when you witnessed a loving embrace). A loving hug is the embodiment of safety, love, and acceptance. You open yourself up to bring someone in, wrap your arms around them, and press that person to you, heart to heart. The best hugs are when you both allow yourself to soften, and in that softening, you find strength and support. Only in softening our hearts and our vulnerability can we touch each other.

Open your arms and embrace that part of you that you are ashamed of. Hold it, love it, speak sweet tender words to it. Let yourself know that you are loved.

When you hold yourself, you allow others to hold you as well. Meet and embrace yourself in your fullness.

Self-Integrate: Love Yourself to Wholeness

> *Amazing Grace,*
> *How sweet the sound*
> *That saved a wretch like me*
> *I once was lost, but now I'm found*
> *Was blind, but now I see*
>
> *'Twas grace that taught my heart to fear*
> *And grace my fears relieved*
> *How precious did that grace appear*
> *The hour I first believed*

I sang "Amazing Grace" when I facilitated an embodiment and empowerment session for an intimate gathering of healing professionals. In the crowd was one of my idols, Dr. Daniel Siegel. He is a clinical professor of psychiatry at the UCLA School of Medicine, and his work on neuroscience and mindfulness meditation enormously influenced my self-love healing journey. I sang this song because I feel that "Amazing Grace" is a melodic and artful rendition of the process of integration, the final step in the journey of self-love.

Dr. Siegel says, "When we are able to 'make sense' of our lives in a deep, integrative manner, what emerges is a coherent narrative of our lives."[13] Integration is when you take all the scattered and hidden pieces of yourself that you saw (Self-Intimacy), embrace (Self-Acceptance), and begin to put them together in a way that feels nourishing, grounding, and whole (Self-Integration).

Shame lives in shadowed darkness, and in this darkness, we have a choice: to face the unknown and dance with the mysterious movements of our soul or be swallowed by the darkness of stagnancy and loss. Shame offers us an

---

[13] Daniel J. Siegel, *Mindsight: the new science of personal transformation.* (New York: Random House, 2010), p.110.

opportunity to speak the language of the heart and claim the pieces of yourself that you disowned.

Integration is granting ourselves amazing grace in how we narrate the story of our lives to ourselves and others. When we allow ourselves to see and accept the parts of us that we hide, we can hear the underlying need: to be loved, exactly as we are. And that starts with us loving ourselves fully, despite and because of our scars, blemishes, mistakes, and shortcomings.

This can happen only when you see and experience yourself as already whole. You are not broken. You are multifaceted, multidimensional, and complex. Integration is choosing to dance with your shadows and your light.

Terry's life changed when she got herpes from her husband, who cheated on her right before leaving their relationship. She was now a single parent of two young children. She felt betrayed, self-loathing, and fear that she would never find love again.

We went on this Self-Love and Sensual Intelligence journey that I am sharing with you.

Terry began her journey feeling completely shut down, not dating, hating her ex, and hating herself. After six months, she blossomed. She felt confident and was better able to navigate the complexities of her relationship. She felt empowered, loved herself, and eventually started dating. She opened to her beauty, power, and sensuality in a way that was never possible before.

The Self-Love journey is powerful. It is a rewriting of the stories in our bodies, hearts, and minds. It is a rebirth. Our rebirth can be clumsy and difficult, yet it is beautiful and perfect.

The song "Amazing Grace" is a promise to ourselves: to lovingly embrace all of who we are. It is an intimate experience where we finally look at ourselves in clear light and claim ourselves. We are not pristine and perfectly packaged, instead we are achingly exquisite and raw.

Chapter 12 Summary

- We heal damaging emotions like shame through Self-Love.
- The steps towards Self-Love are Self-Intimacy, Self-Acceptance, and Self-Integration.
- Self-Intimacy is looking at yourself, including the difficult parts. Self-Acceptance is embracing who you are without judgment. Self-Integration grants us the grace to create our life narrative that includes our wholeness.
- Sit in your seat of power, pleasure, and peace. Embrace yourself and be in a conscious relationship with your core and the lifeblood that runs through your body.

Chapter 13

CALM YOUR MIND

Mind's Natural Abilities + Awareness Practice = Mindfulness

A Sensual Mind

I don't know how to be sexy...
But I do know how to
Enjoy every word that comes out of my mouth
The slippery tumble of
Nouns, pronouns, verbs, adverbs, adjectives, prepositions, conjunctions, interjections
As they twist and curl around themselves around my tongue.
I feel their peeking, shy, exploring, then touching, grabbing, fumbling
Oh did you mean to touch right there?
What a delicious little accident of sensation and meaning as
These words
Dance and shake,
Dominate and undulate.
As they gyrate their way all over my tongue, my teeth, my lips,
Giving meaning to the hot saliva in my cheeks,
That turns into spit when these words leave the heat of my hot body vessel,
Expelled by the sucking and blowing movement of my lungs
These words...
Raw, unfiltered, naked, exposed
Out into the cold open air
Loving the sensation of apprehension
In the crackling silence
As they caress and press against
And onto
And Into
Ears
And touch the minds of those not yet certain if they're ready to hear what they heard.

Pop quiz time!

13 + 34 = ?

Which of the five is least like the other four?

1. Parrot
2. Raven
3. Penguin
4. Hawk
5. Sparrow

You're playing "Pin the tail on the donkey." Before being blindfolded, you see you are facing east. You are spun 180 degrees to the right, then 720 degrees to the left. In what direction are you now facing?

1. North
2. South
3. East
4. West

Congratulations, we just exercised some of our mind's natural ability! Problem-solving, creating order, and cognition are some of the most valued assets one can possess in western society. The mind is also the tool that's supposed to keep us in line and productive.

So, why do people tell me, "I need to get out of my head and into my body!"? If utilizing the mind is the height of ability, why do so many people feel limited, dull, sad, numb, and uninspired? Why does it feel difficult to be with ourselves? Why do our incessant thoughts take over and make us miserable?

It's because we've been taught an over-reliance on just a few functions of the mind: cognition, problem-solving, and order-making. This leads to feeling trapped by our habituated thought patterns, making the same decisions, and getting stuck in the same old circumstances.

Arthur Fleming, the former head of the United Negro College Fund, coined, "A mind is a terrible thing to waste." This is true. Our feeling of stuckness in our heads doesn't come from the mind itself but how we use the mind. We do not use the mind to its fullest capacity.

The *underutilized* mind is a dangerous place to be.

So, what can we do?

Mindfulness is the third component of sensual intelligence. Mindfulness is the mind's natural abilities plus awareness practice. In *Mindsight*, Daniel Seigel says, "Inviting our thoughts and feelings into awareness allows us to learn from them rather than be driven by them. We can calm them without ignoring them; we can hear their wisdom without being terrified by their screaming voices."[14] We take ourselves off of autopilot by allowing our thoughts but not taking them at face value and being controlled by our thoughts and whims. We begin to change our lives and actions.

Our brains and habits aren't static—they are plastic, meaning they can be changed. Mindfulness is how we use the mind's natural abilities and awareness practice. We use mindfulness to make sense of the world and our place in it. Mindfulness and awareness allow us to tap into the mind's capacity to enhance itself by training new habits and beliefs. This is available through the connection between body intelligence (embodied awareness) and the heart.[15]

---

[14] Daniel J. Siegel, *Mindsight: the new science of personal transformation.* (New York: Random House, 2010), p. 16.

[15] Check out the fields of Heart Math and mindfulness meditation for in-depth understanding of the neural connections in the heart, and how we can train the mind. This is a link to the Heart Math Institute: https://www.heartmath.org. Mindfulness and meditation books and

I suffered from depression for many years. Depression felt like "The Swamp of Sadness" from my favorite childhood movie, *The Neverending Story:* a foggy, gray marsh with thick, heavy, waist-high mud. If you stopped moving, the sadness would suck you under, and you would drown in your own misery. I experienced this every single day. I was functional and productive when I had to be, but I had no joy, drive, or hope.

One day, during a deep depression, I was in the shower, and out of nowhere, a voice said, "Stop being so mean to me!" I gasped. It was the voice of a child, but there was no child in that bathroom with me. There was no one there but me. That child's voice, filled with pain, was literally my voice. My inner child's voice escaped from the core of my belly and out of my mouth, laced with despair and misery.

As soon as that voice said, "Stop being so mean to me," I finally—*truly*—heard the dark, grumbling, vile voices that were always talking inside my head, telling me everything I was doing wrong, detailing every shortcoming. "You're not good enough. You're not doing enough. What are you even thinking? You're never going to make it! You're lazy. You suck! You need to do better!"

On and on and on these voices tore me apart, until something from the depths of me begged the voices to stop.

It was just like that moment in *Horton Hears a Who* when finally, everyone hears a big "Yopp" from one of the tiny Whos living in Whoville. It came from the tiniest Who of all. The child part of us, the innocent, loving, trusting, and tender part of us that gets trampled on in our journey of striving ambition, of fitting in, of doing it right—or, if not right, then making it seem so.

Before this moment, it never occurred to me that I was hurting myself. I always felt like I had to push to perform better and be better. I didn't know *I* made it such a dangerous place inside my own head. I didn't realize I had any other choice.

---

resources I have used include books by Cheri Huber, Jon Kabat-Zinn, and Thich Nhat Hanh. These authors have been my guides.

This is how the loop of the unintegrated mind, body, and heart looks like: You have an experience, then you feel something about it. Then, you judge yourself about how you feel. Then you feel something else about the judgment you just made, and then you judge that and feel something else, and so on and so on. It's a downward spiral.

It is an unnerving experience when you hear different parts of yourself expressing different opinions on your life. Our bodies and our minds can operate separately—isn't that interesting? We can divide into parts, so much so that a part of ourselves is unaware of other parts of ourselves.

SIP
Mindfulness Practice

Connect yourself to your senses and get in touch with your sensual intelligence. Be mindful of what you can taste, touch, smell, hear, and see in your own body, in your cells, in how you move in the world, in how you move with yourself, in how you breathe.

Don't just envision the world you want to create. Embody it. You can train the mind by training yourself to feel the things you have ignored.

Sometimes it can be hard to tell what is actually ours and what has been scripted to us. Let's take, for example, the idea of "success ." What does success *actually* look like for us? What does it actually *feel* like? There is an "out there" idea of what a successful career, partnership, body type, and standard of beauty look like. It was a big deal when I shaved my hair off at 18 because the script says "long hair is beautiful ." It is a sign of desirability, femininity, and success as a woman.

When I decided to dance and be an artist instead of a consultant after attending a top-tier college, I felt the pressure of the script. Was going to work for a corporation, getting a fat paycheck, drinking with colleagues at happy hour, and renting a swank downtown apartment the successful thing to do? Was I a failure for choosing freedom of expression and renting a little room in a family home?

It can be hard to tell because we become unconsciously shaped by our conditioning and social structures that keep us doing the "right" thing. What are the thoughts in our heads that reflect our true values? Are we acting from a place of self-love, groundedness, and alignment, or are we reacting in collusion or rebelling?

Mindfulness gives us the gift of consciousness. It offers a slowing down, paying attention, the ability to just be with ourselves and our thoughts as a rushing river, as the waves of the ocean. And instead of trying to escape, control, or change the thoughts, we just allow them to be. We learn to align to the truth of ourselves as it changes from situation to situation. It is a constant attuning and aligning to our fundamental values.

This is the invitation to learn to anchor ourselves in stillness and calm as the waves of our thoughts pass through us. It takes practice and dedication, but it is healing integration.

Chapter 13 Summary

- We've been taught an overreliance on the analytical, problem-solving functions of the brain. This leads to feeling "stuck in our heads" because our habituated thoughts trap us.
- Mindfulness allows us to be with the thoughts and let them go, rather than be driven by them.
- We use embodiment and focus on the breath to be with our thoughts without ignoring them, so we can hear our internal wisdom without being overwhelmed by the voices in our heads.

Chapter 14

COMMUNITY

Other Bodies + Environment = Community

Sensual Intelligence is communication between our body, our expression, and others, including nature itself. The intelligence of sensuality comes from the interplay between all of us, sharing what is real, what is felt. When we share and participate in the community, we add to each other's experiences and create deeply relational, nourishing spaces for growth.

Community is our playground. It offers us the opportunity to play and interact, see and be seen, share triumphs and shortcomings, and know that we can be perfectly imperfect and always become more of who we are meant to be.

To heal our community, we have to start with ourselves so that we can fully participate in collective healing. We exist and grow in a community, so we heal through our collective energy, collectively honoring our grief, fear, anger, and sadness. We use movement to transmute and transmit, digging down into the depths of our knowledge.

We can change the world by healing our relationships with our bodies and sensuality. The journey of Sensual Intelligence is about becoming aware of your body, learning to love yourself, and expressing yourself authentically. As you reclaim yourself, you begin to have the skills to sense the nuance with your community. You can create loving boundaries and compassion and still fully, truthfully express yourself.

However, even a relatively healthy community can have its problems. You must make sure you are able to interact with your community appropriately and safely.

How can you tell what an appropriate form of interaction is? It must involve these four things: attunement, communication, consent, and mindfulness.

Attunement: Are you able to sense what the person's body language, facial expression, etc., are telling you?

Communication: Are you able and willing to articulate your feelings, be it verbal or nonverbal?

Consent: Are you both in agreement with what is going on?

Mindfulness: Are you honoring the agreements made by society, your company, your relationships?

Violations happen when one or more of these conditions are not met. We're humans, so we are going to mess up. However, without compassion, we can too quickly and definitively shut out people who really would benefit from not only being included but would deeply enrich the beauty of the community. Chapter 12, Self-Love, spoke about integrating the parts that we have left behind and feel shame around. In a community, this same act is called inclusion: including people that we have left behind and feel shame around. It is the same process. It is not easy. It is not simple. It will take great courage; it will take other-intimacy, other-acceptance, and other-integration to heal and create community. By this, I mean that we extend intimacy, acceptance, and integration beyond ourselves, beyond our bodies, to include others. But the first step towards doing this authentically is to create it within yourself first.

After being rejected and punished multiple times with no actual teaching and rehabilitation, some community violators eventually give up trying to get their basic needs met through collaborative, cooperative community interactions. The cost of violating someone else to get what they need is worth the cost since they do not know any alternative.

Sensual Intelligence practices help us become comfortable with our bodies, power, and communication, allowing us the space and skill to offer others the same spaciousness and understanding. Shaming each other for trying and/or failing makes it unsafe to try again.

SQ is a way to bring us back together and connect us to ourselves and each other. When you heal yourself, you also heal the community, your family, your loved ones, your work.

The Power of Being Witnessed

The Witnesses

We just need permission to be ourselves and to know that we are held.
I invite you to ignore anyone who does not encourage you to come back to yourself.
Anyone who will not be there to help you release shame and unleash the amazing creature that you are
Because you are an amazing creature.
You are beauty and perfection incarnate
You are a perfect being
Your stories and how they shaped you
And how you watched them shape you
And even how they made you gnarled, hardened, and angry,

*We witness you in those beautiful, powerful, raw emotions
And we know you will allow them to soften you into the wise being that you are.*

*My love,
Turn off the shoulda and coulda and woulda
And dance with yourself
In silence.
In reverie.
Worship your vessel, your body, your being.
BE with yourself as if in prayer.
Let yourself be
And you will hear your body and intuition whisper to you.
And you will find a place that provides a space for you to see,
Feel, celebrate, and encourage
All of who you are.
And you will feel the truth, the power, the quiet and calm knowing of who you are,
That no person, no class, no guru can give to you
Other than you.
So breathe and be
And be and breathe
And open yourself wide
And swallow yourself whole
And rest your head on your own loving heart
And hold yourself dear
And let yourself run free
and make the promises that you know you will keep.
The promises of:
"I am here with you
However you are
In the deep, in the fear, in the beauty, in the shit, in the revelations, in the descent to darkness, In the rigidity, in the loss, in the friendships forged, and the friendships torn apart.
I am here with you."
Be in deep communion with yourself and heal.*

> *We will guide, witness, and celebrate*
> *You becoming more of you*
> *Embracing all of you.*
>
> *We are the witnesses*
> *Here to help you see yourself,*
> *To Mourn when you lose yourself,*
> *To Love when you find yourself again.*
> *We are your mirrors.*
>
> *It is an honor to see you,*
> *And to be seen.*

When we are in community we get to witness our different journeys and be mirrors for one another. Every single one of our bodies has a different experience of the world. Society treats and perceives each of our beautiful bodies very differently. Age, ethnicity, religion, profession, marital status, and more create a unique experience, some form of role expectation, or stereotype. We hold in our bones the history and trauma of our ancestors. We experience the world through the stories the world gives us and how we embody these stories in our community.

As I grew in my healing journey, my relationship with my mom dramatically changed. She is a social worker, so I have a soft spot in my heart for all social service workers, people who deal with humanity directly and have to experience the dark and ugly parts of humanity daily. She told me that I inspired her to keep growing and keep trying. My growth inspired her to grow, too.

She is a social worker, so I have a soft spot in my heart for all social service workers, people who deal with humanity directly and have to experience the dark and ugly parts of humanity daily.

I facilitated small groups of women social workers, where we could be more intimate and overt about the benefits of pleasure and sensuality in decreasing stress. It was *so cute* to see my mom get all sexy on the fold-out chairs and giggle in front of the other social workers. (My mom is not a giggler!) Later, she told me that they all felt more energetic and happy about the job and connected to their bodies. If these women can find joy in their stressful jobs, you can, too!

The goal is always the same, no matter who I am working with: to create a sense of community and connection. I've worked with police, tech and government workers, entrepreneurs, holistic health practitioners, educators, youth of all ages, supervisors, lawyers, managers, and caseworkers. I use the same concepts you find here in this book.

I like to let the audience know the mechanisms behind the activities I facilitate and how these things create new neural networks (because of neuroplasticity) in the brain. I facilitate the content and concepts of SQ without telling the participants its name. People do not realize that their lack of SQ is driving the discomfort and disconnection from themselves, their colleagues, and their work.

Work environments are some of the most difficult yet most rewarding areas to facilitate SQ exercises. Here I will share about community and the power of being witnessed.

Remember this chant?

I am power. Hear me roar!
I love my body, so I can soar.
I know my mind, ideas so bright,
I speak from my heart and shine my light.

I use that chant in my large groups and then go into this share:

> Okay everybody, let's split into two groups:
> 1. Group A and Group B.
> 2. Go to opposite sides of the room.
> 3. Face each other.
> 4. Look.

These are your people, your colleagues, your friends across the room. See them.

When we come together, we are a collection of heartbeats and breaths. We are going to witness each other in our fullness. Group A, you are the heartbeat, the breath, the rhythm. You're going to stomp and clap and give Group B all your love and encouragement.

Group B, I want you to open and feel the encouragement, the rhythm. Let it fill up your entire body. Then you are going to walk, no, *strut* your fabulous self toward Group A. Show them, announce to them the truth of your being. Then we are going to switch.

This is what community is for: to lift each other and witness and encourage our greatness and beauty.

They get their heart rates up, they move as one heartbeat, as one family, they laugh, they hug, and it is beautiful. We create a sense of community as it is meant to be: not judgmental or competitive, but embodied and proud in their bodies.

The second part of this facilitation, which is a deeper part of witnessing the heart, is called the "River of Appreciation."

Choose one person who is going to go first. The chosen person, you are going to face your three colleagues. Make sure your hands are down at your sides. The *only* thing you get to do is receive. Just be open and receive.

Everyone else is going to look at the chosen person, and I want you to share with them what you see in them. Not what they are wearing, not how they look. Acknowledge how you see them, how you experience them. Look at their heart. Even if you don't know them, you can still see who they are, their heart, contribution to the world, vulnerability, and gifts. Tell them.

The chosen person, remember, you stand there, arms down to your sides, palms open and facing up. The only thing you do is stand there and receive.

And then you will switch, and everyone will acknowledge and will be acknowledged.

While this exercise seems very simple, the power of transformation is in simplicity. The majority of us have had to shove down our feelings and our need for appreciation—to where no one can see them, even ourselves. Our simple humanity may not have been given space to exist without judgment.

Multiple participants over the years have shared that they have *never* felt acknowledged or seen or appreciated for who they are and what they do.

People cry. They open. They are seen. It is magnificent.

Give this exercise a try! If not with your workplace, do it with your friends or family, or even with yourself in the mirror.

Intimate Witnessing

The Sensual Intelligence journeyers are always incredibly diverse. They range in age from 20s to 60s, consisting of students, therapists, entrepreneurs, corporate workers, artists, and educators. They identify as Asian, Latinx, White, Black; Jewish, Christian, spiritual, and more. One group met right in the middle of everything 2020 had to offer: Black Lives Matter demonstrations, mask-mandate protests, and an extraordinarily intense presidential election, in addition to being shut in their homes for months.

That time was a rite of passage. We explored power dynamics, privilege, and individual experiences through the lens of sensuality. We asked questions like, "What is the role of pleasure in the social justice movement?" and "How do you stay embodied when the world feels like a scary place for the body to be?" We did not just ask these questions and talk them through. We used the principles of Sensual Intelligence to guide our search for inner and outer peace.

Through moaning and groaning, creating a healing circle around one person, and reflecting their groans of pleasure, fear, sadness, and ecstasy. Following the movement of their body as they explore the expression of themselves: their eroticism, pain, shame, confusion. We hold each person even in their trepidation, fears, and insecurities. They enter the middle of the sacred circle, and we witness as they break open into their rawness.

It was incredibly potent and a testament to the importance of this work. One participant shared, "All I can say is, I wish I had taken this course earlier in my life. I feel I have never spent such necessary time in the course of my healing. My life will never be the same, and I am grateful for that."

We will often have circles that witness each other in our pain, but not many witness each other in pleasure, beauty, passion, and celebration. Yet, that is what we all need: a space of encouragement and non-judgment in exploring who we really are, as opposed to the need for performance to be accepted as good enough. The realm of play invites us into this world of exploration, imagination, and creation.

Beauty and pleasure and the sublime act of self-expression, acceptance, and celebration by the community can help us find ourselves, feel ourselves, express ourselves, and share that internal journey with others. Sharing yourself is a generous act.

We are born into love and exuberance for life, unabashed and wild. We then get pushed into fear, shame, self-hatred, and abandonment. We abandon our true selves to be perceived as important, welcome, OK.

The pathway to being self-fulfilled lies in feeling yourself being celebrated and accepted in the community. We witness and are witnessed in our internal and shared journeys.

Environment

> Nature Prayers
>
> *Unwinding, slow grinding my prayers into the hot, hot sand,*
> *My dark skin caressed and blessed by the heat of the bright yellow sun*
> *The earth is my lover, my mother, my muse*
> *I listen to her slow beautiful song*
> *While I bathe in the salted ocean breeze And let the water wash over me*
> *Wash over me*
> *Wash over me*
>
> (I danced this poem on the beach in Maui. You can watch it on my Instagram account @shawnreynotto). Or just go to http://www.Shawnrey.com/book-resources for this and other book resources.

Nature and sensuality are irreconcilably linked. Being in our Sensual Intelligence is so much more than about the self. It is about recognizing and experiencing self as a part of nature. We are of the natural world, and what we do to ourselves, we also do to the environment.

Gaia, Pachamama, Mother Earth are the names we give to this planet we live on, where all of our sensual embodied existences play out. All of these names for the earth have a feminine, mothering, nurturing energy. We are held in the womb, and we are the children playing. The earth herself moves with weather systems, joints creaking with every seismic shifting of tectonic plates. We can never separate ourselves, our lives, from this living organism that we live on and contribute to. We live on a planet that is in a delicate balancing dance with all of the life forms.

Pleasure, paying attention to the senses, connecting to our human spirit and desire, is an act of rewilding and unlocking our Sensual Intelligence. When we tend to our bodies, we tend to the earth. When we care for the earth, we care for our bodies. When we disconnect from ourselves, bodies, and the land, we forget what brings us actual pleasure outside of what has been allowed.

Sensual Intelligence is the ultimate path to understanding that we are inextricably woven together. Through the senses of the body, we feel the sensuality of this planet. Our bodies are an entire ecosystem that mirrors our life in our environment.

Earth herself is the manifestation of Sensual Intelligence. If we hold our sensuality in regard and relation, we are much less likely to destroy what sustains us. We've been taught to see the earth as something dangerous, something to be controlled and exploited. Instead, we need to recognize that the earth is our source of nourishment, which gives us so much care *and* needs to be cared for.

You are breath. You are life. You are joy embodied! So, open your arms wide and your smile even wider, and let yourself be a portal of love. Let Gaia pour into you and out of you with every breath. Joy is not given to us; it is created from us and delivered through us in our relationships with each other and our planet. We are sensual beings, smelling, tasting, touching, hearing, and seeing the gifts of this world.

Chapter 14 Summary

- Community is Other Bodies + Environment.
- Our environment, especially nature, is part of an ecosystem of sustainability and regeneration. Sensual Intelligence allows us to participate in our world responsibly.
- Connecting to the intelligence of the community allows you to create loving boundaries and compassion and still truthfully express yourself.
- To have healthy community interactions, we must practice attunement, communication, consent, and mindfulness.
- The pathway to being self-fulfilled lies in feeling yourself being witnessed and accepted in the community.

Chapter 15

CONSENT AND CONSENSUAL COMMUNITY

Dance Your Life

I miss dancing.
Specifically partner dancing.
I miss leaning into and pulling away from another's body, our hands linked.
Feeling our heat, our sweat, the ever-changing swirl, dip, and sway in the conversation of our forms.

My body has been talking to herself a lot lately. And while this is totally fine (I give her sweet whispers, great shouts, and groans), I miss being able to touch another person, roll our hips, and bring ourselves alive from the inside out with just our breathing.

> *I miss speaking to another body in dance.*
> *I miss the mingling of our sweat.*
> *I miss the deep listening to and delicious pressing against my boundaries.*
>
> *Dance is such an exquisite, sensual playground for exploring pleasure, my "yes," my "no," my strength, my surrender, my giving, my receiving.*
> *Because the best partner dance is actually deep listening. Deep listening to your own body and to their body.*
> *And through that listening, you get to create a world, a secret, unique conversation, that only the two of you can have.*
> *And then another partner, another language, another world.*
> *And then another.*
> *And then another.*
> *And another…*
> *In dancing with others my body, my cells, my expression gets spoken to life in so many different ways.*
> *And I listen to their story and the expression of their bodies.*
>
> *I miss partner dancing.*
> *I miss talking to your body.*
> *I miss you listening to my body.*

Consent is not "sexy." Consent is *sensual*.

It is no mistake that "sensual" is in the word consensual. You cannot have consent without sensuality. Literally translated, consensual means: with the senses. Consent without the sensual is like a car with no engine. It will not run. You have to be in touch with your own body and your Sensual IQ to connect with another person and create a consensual agreement.

Consent should feel like a celebration in your body and all of those involved. It is a consensus of being, where you feel both safety and expansion. It is the delight that blossoms inside you when you attune and align with your body's desires and intentions with that of another person, sentient being, group, situation, or environment.

So, consent starts with yourself.

When we are not connected to ourselves, it is hard to create the dance of consent. Many people have not truly taken the time to feel themselves, their bodies, and their true desires. Many of us have not asked ourselves, "How does this feel? Do I like it? Is it nourishing?" If we have not gotten confirmation on these questions, how can we have consent with ourselves? When we are not in a conscious relationship with ourselves, other people can play us and act on our behalf, in their self-interest. We violate ourselves, each other, and the community by not implementing self-consent.

When parts of yourself go unconscious, they slip out and express themselves, unbeknownst. I call this leakage. You see leakage a lot in various ways:

- Micro-aggression.
- Sudden turns of temper.
- Seeking touch and connection in ways that violate people's boundaries.

This is why teaching consent culture without teaching people how to connect with their bodies is irresponsible. This leads to confusion, struggle, or resistance because this tries to get people to intellectually understand the rules and facts about consent without feeling it in their bodies. That's not how consent is created. Consent is made, felt, and expressed in and through the body.

Rape, sexual assault, sexual harassment, molestation all have one thing in common: there is no consent. One possible cause of root of sexual harassment is an unconscious, untrained, and misplaced bid for connection. When embodied expression (including sensuality) is repressed, it gets distorted. Sensuality, for example, warps into inappropriate sexual expression. I spoke about this in the "Speed and Spice: Sensuality is NOT Sex" section in Chapter 4.

So what about people who think they got consent from you, but they actually have not?

Tell them.

This book focuses on making sure you are clear and empowered in yourself. The more clear and empowered you are within yourself, the less time you have for bullshit. You cannot control other people, their actions, or their thoughts, but you have power over your own.[16]

I had an encounter with a man who called me childish after I told him that I would be open to hanging out with him only as friends. Specifically, I said: "I don't mind a friendly get-together. I'm not into making out or anything. I'm just here to enjoy friendships, nature, and magic. So if that's good with you, then yes."

I did two things with this message: I named his leaking sexual energy and set my engagement boundary. (Learn more about Boundaries in Chapter 22, Power).

I'm a sensuality and embodiment coach who identifies as a woman, and I have physical attributes that our current society's beauty standards deem as "attractive." I have a lot of experience doing energetic aikido with unwanted advances. I felt the underlying desire and responded honestly, respectfully, and immediately. I can tell when someone is being friendly and when someone is "leaking." He assumed he was approaching me with innocence

---

[16] As a black woman, I am well aware of the atrocities of systemic racism, oppression, sexism, modern slavery, trafficking, and the very real danger that plagues people who have been made invisible and/or marginalized for their gender, ethnicity, faith, ability, class, and employment. Police brutality, bigoted vigilantism, gerrymandering, punishing victims of sexual abuse, and more, are all examples flagrant disregard of consent, and an embrace of violence.

These are very real, systemic problems that cannot be willed away simply by knowing yourself. There are very real perpetrators who are born into and benefit from our current system. A system that was born out of oppression. However, implementing self-sovereignty is still an incredibly potent practice.

and friendship. This man was leaking, and he didn't know it. So I set a boundary in which consent could happen.

Had his intentions truly been honest and congruent, he would have said something to the effect of, "Oh, yes, absolutely. You're a cool person. I'm 100 percent excited to hang out, just friendship. Perfect!"

Instead, he waited a month before responding to my message and said: "Obviously, it's taken me a while to respond to this, but it's the most childish response I've ever gotten just to try to get together with someone I thought was cool. I haven't heard the term 'making out' since I was 15 years old. I guess I was wrong. Namaste."

This is what happens when something in the shadows gets suddenly exposed: name-calling; passive aggression; lack of compassion; no curiosity, honor, or respect.

I have had too many non-consensual encounters with people (in my case, cis-gender, hetero-men, since I am a cis-gendered,[17] mostly hetero woman) in the conscious dance scene and conscious intimacy workshops. I experienced many people who, quite frankly, have just been mentally masturbating and aggrandizing themselves. They will come up to me and tell me that they felt a connection, and they will look longingly into my eyes, and say: "I feel so connected to you. We're connected. I can feel it."

First of all, no. Second of all, no.

What they felt was an *attraction*. Attraction, desire, and turn-on are powerful, beautiful energies that light us up and inspire us! However, attraction is a one-way street. Attraction does not indicate a connection.

Connection is a more complex highway that needs at least two people to consensually agree that there is a mutual affinity. Then, and *only* then, can

---

[17] Cisgender: of, relating to, or being a person whose gender identity corresponds with the sex the person had or was identified as having at birth". Merriam-Webster.com Dictionary, Merriam-Webster, https://www.merriam-webster.com/dictionary/cisgender. Accessed 9 Nov. 2021.

you start to have a "connection." Before that, it's premature. It's a one-way attraction. Period.

bell hooks made this point infinitely clear in her book, *All About Love: New Visions*, when she said, "I am often struck by the dangerous narcissism fostered by spiritual rhetoric that pays too much attention to individual self-improvement and so little to the practice of love within the context of community."[18] Community is created through a series of connections. Connection takes listening, and it needs spaciousness, safety, and trust. Be humble. We're not gods and goddesses. We're just people with pieces of god inside of us, and having those pieces of God light up when we truly share in community.

We will have miscommunications and misunderstandings, and just like novices in a partner dance class, we will step on toes and bump foreheads. This is the nature of being a human, creating connections and community. Sensual Intelligence tools help you be the most aligned, empowered, sovereign, sensual human you can be.

Consent is alive as much as our bodies are alive. It is a living contract, one that dances in the space of body to body, of will to will, of intention to intention. Our connection to our bodies is critical to every agreement: professional, romantic, and beyond. It requires a deep knowing, cherishing, and honoring of self. We cannot understand what we do not take the time to know. We cannot take care of what we do not cherish. We cannot respect what we do not honor.

We will not train the world in a day. We will still encounter people who try to trample our boundaries and then call us names for standing up for ourselves. But what is most important is that you can stay in your center, your power, your joy, and not let some bullshit make you feel unworthy of respect. The

---

[18] bell hooks. *All About Love: New Visions*. (New York: Harper Collins Publishers, 2001), p. 108).

purpose of this book is to remind you in a million different ways and to help you embody deep in the marrow of your bones an important message.

Say this out loud to yourself: "I am worthy. I am valuable. I'm fucking awesome and only need to surround myself with people who can reflect that."

Chapter 15 Summary

- Consent is not sexy; it is Consensual.
- Con + Sensual = Consensual. Con = with. Consent *must* have sensuality.
- Consent starts with creating consent with yourself. The only way to get consent from yourself is to know yourself. You get to know yourself through sensual intelligence.
- Consent has coherent, integrated, embodied communication with the senses.

SIP
Create Your Consensual Dance

How do you create a consensual dance with yourself?

Move when you feel moved.

So many times, we will move or act because it is the "right" thing to do. It follows the order of how things are supposed to happen. It's habitual. It's custom. It's what everyone else is doing.

No. Stop that.

Creating a consensual dance means you have to feel yourself and only move when you genuinely feel moved.

Turn on your favorite music.

Listen to it. Feel what the music has to say to your soul. If the song makes you feel like it is time to sit down and cry, feel it deeply in your bones, then sit down and cry. If you feel the music invites you to move only occasionally, only move occasionally.

Let go of any idea of how it is supposed to be and practice feeling it. That is consensual.

Feel strong, capable, in love with, and connect with the beauty of your unique body: your physical body, emotional body, and spiritual body. Create yourself as living poetry, for poetry is not linear and neither are you. Allow the poetry of your body to dance and frolic, to create rhymes, rhythms, beats, and undulations that honor and respect the ever-changing flow of your being. Taste, touch, smell, listen, see the healing of you. This creates a web of sensuality of your own making. Allow your body to move freely, as it needs, not as everyone else wants.

This is the path of Sensual Intelligence, a step towards building a consensual world.

Part 3:

YOUR SENSUAL EXPRESSION JOURNEY

Children of the Stars

You are everything:
All the elements, all the energies, all the pleasure and the joy
Be the poetry,
Dance the healing,
Claim your voice,
Embody your bliss.
Live the poetry of your life.
Walk the beauty of your surroundings.
Absorb the blessings that come your way.
Empower yourself with the gifts of your body.
Bow to the strength of your own heart and stand in awe of
your own vast potency.
Welcome children of the earth, seas, wind, and stars.

Chapter 16

THE 7Ps OF SENSUAL EXPRESSION

Sensual Intelligence is all about discovering your innate gifts and developing the tools that will allow you to have a safe, joyful, and nourishing relationship with your body, wherever you are, in whatever situation. To do that, we have the 7Ps of Sensual Expression. Each of the 7Ps has intelligence that informs us how to see, think, and act in the world.

The 7Ps of Sensual Expression work together to bring support and balance to our lives. Having a conscious, balanced relationship with all aspects of ourselves means having the tools and wherewithal to choose what we're up to in life. If you do not have a balanced relationship with Power, for example, you're not going to use it with consistency and awareness. So throughout this work, we're going to start consciously and deliberately discovering and then, hopefully, integrating these parts of ourselves.

I will include a table showing how this Sensual Expression in the components of the Sensual body: Embodiment, Self-Love, Mindfulness, and Community.

Embodiment (Body)	How we are in our bodies and how we use our bodies. **Balanced**: Connective & nourishing. **Unbalanced**: Painful & disconnected.
Self-Love (Heart)	How we feel about ourselves. Our relationship to heart, emotions. **Balanced**: Heart/emotions nourishing. **Unbalanced**: Heart/emotions harming and limiting.
Mindfulness (Mind)	What thoughts do we think to rationalize our way of being? What questions do we ask ourselves? What are we trying to solve?
Community (Environment)	How we interact with and contribute to our environment and others.

Some of these expressions will feel completely foreign, and some are all too familiar. Let it all be right! Sensual Intelligence is the invitation to explore both the pain and joy to learn to bring more profound growth in all of life. Gaining the sensual gifts from our pain is just as important as being open to the sensual gifts of pleasure.

When I volunteered in Liberia, one of their favorite dishes was the "bitter ball." True to its name, the bitter ball was an extremely bitter type of eggplant, popular in Liberian dishes. I'll never forget what a young woman told me, with the biggest smile on her face, "I love the bitter ball because it makes the water taste so sweet!" If you dare to feel all of your life as a sensual gift giving you the full spectrum of life's offerings, then you have truly found your way to transform yourself and the world. The journey of Sensual Intelligence is learning how we can honor and dance with the complexity of our existence.

Use the rest of this book to explore all aspects of yourself, your desires, and sensuality without feeling it has to look a certain way. I know that we can feel prohibited from and embarrassed by exploring our bodies and expression. So any time you feel silly, awkward, too loud, too much, or too little, you're not. You're perfect.

Often, adult awkwardness comes when we allow our unfiltered, genuine self to come out in the world. It feels awkward not because it is wrong or bad, but because it's new and fresh, like a butterfly emerging from its cocoon. Butterflies don't come out fully ready to fly. Their wings are wet, drooping, and, well, awkward. And this is perfect. This is normal. You're OK. You're in the right place.

Whether you do this with yourself in the mirror or with a group of friends, you've got this! Reclaim your body, freedom, self-expression, and liberate yourself from the painful, limiting cycle of shaming and policing. You will emerge powerfully and uniquely you. This journey is about your body. Not your job, your mother or father, your children, your failures, or your "shortcomings." It is time to remember your body, beauty, and potency.

Chapter 16 Summary

- The 7Ps of Sensual Expression are Pleasure, Play, Passion, Psyche, Philosophy, Power, and Peace.
- They are the different ways we occupy and use our bodies, how we feel about ourselves and our relationship to our emotions, what thoughts we think to rationalize our way of being, and how we interact with and contribute to our community.
- Your desires, sensuality, and expression do not have to look a certain way to be right.
- Use the 7Ps to get to know yourself and give yourself permission to heal and be fully self-expressed.

Chapter 17

PLEASURE –
THE JOURNEY
OF DELIGHT AND DESIRE

Pleasure's Presence

Pleasure saunters down the stairs,
Her shoulders bared,
The golden-yellow ruffles of her silk dress flirting with the air
As she smiles
And runs her hands along the banister.
She looks you straight in the eyes and says,
"Mmmm, slow down, honey.
Smell the roses.
Feel the beautiful majesty of your body
And the gift of your surroundings.
You, too, are Pleasure."

Element: Earth

Characteristics: Lush, inviting, indulging, loves beauty

Associated SQ Type: The Sensualist

Embodied Sound: Oooo

Embodied Gesture: Head back, mouth open, with a slow and decadent caress from the throat to the core of the body

Motto: Slow Down and Savor

Embodiment (Body)	**Body Language**: Body prominent. Unhurried. Slower body movements to savor the moment. Moans, groans, and other sounds of satisfaction.
	Balanced: Loves the body and cares for it. Sees self in nature and as a part of nature. Lush, inviting, alluring.
	Unbalanced: Over-indulgent. gluttonous, hedonist, can get addicted to love, sex, looks.
Self-Love (Heart)	**Balanced**: Romantic, generous with love and compliments. Experiences beauty, sensual
	Unbalanced: Indulgent, hedonist, abandons self to get pleasure or romance. Use their body to distract from difficult feelings. Difficulty being alone, not admired, ordinary, responsible, and burdened with obligation.
Mindfulness (Mind)	**Balanced**: "How do I bring delight and beauty? "
	Sees the sensual and possibility of beauty in everything. Poetic languaging. Allows an experience to unfold and pays attention to details that delight.
	Unbalanced: "What about *me*? What about *my* physical needs?"
	Vain, shallow, needs external validation of beauty, desirability. Self-absorbed especially around subjects of dating, relationships, looks, and/or sex.

Community	**Balanced**: Brings beauty, appreciation. Helps us be in the moment and present. Embodies connection with environment, experiences nature as not separate from human experience.
	Unbalanced: Uses body, beauty, pleasure, and touch to manipulate to get what they want. This creates jealousy, cattiness, discord to bring attention and comfort to themselves.

A Pleasure Story...

You get up, and you have nothing planned. You languidly ask yourself, "What am I a 'yes' to today? What am I a 'no' to today? You pause and feel deeply into your body for the answer. This spaciousness is like honey and sweetness dripping down your spine. You step outside onto the porch for 'me-time.' The sun warms your skin, and you surrender to your senses. You are in the present moment, and you feel alive. You take a deep breath and sigh, swaying and moving your body, feeling grounded, open, and receptive.

Everything else around you fades away. There is no feeling lost in your thoughts, stresses, worries, or anxieties. You do what is authentic and allow the moment to take whatever form it takes. You feel subtle yet bold, bright, and full of beautiful light.

You are in Pleasure. To be in Pleasure is to live in the beauty of the heart.

The Cambridge Dictionary defines pleasure as "a feeling of enjoyment or satisfaction."[19] But Pleasure is so much more than that. Pleasure is not just a feeling, and it is not just a noun. It is an unfolding, a becoming and discovering

---

[19] "Pleasure." https://dictionary.Cambridge.org/us/. Cambridge Academic Content Dictionary, 2021. Web 29 November 2021.

of self along the way. We've been taught to treat pleasure as something to have, but Pleasure is a journey, not a destination. It is the process of embodied delights: earthy, appreciative, savoring, and indulgent.

Before being repressed, we were sensual creatures, indulging in the sensual pleasures of life and the pure being of our bodies. To truly understand the journey of Pleasure, we have to go back to its ancient origins. There we find that Pleasure is the daughter of Eros and Psyche.

Eros (also known as Cupid) is the embodiment of desire, movement, and creative force. It is the yearning inside of us which compels us to move, create, blossom, and explore. When Cupid's bow pricks us, we see the world for all of its gifts and cannot help but be drawn to their splendor. We are moved and inspired, pulled into a world of infinite and exquisite longing.

Psyche (also known as Anima) is the personification of the human spirit. Sensitive, pure, and loving, Psyche is the pure essence of our soul and the depths of our understanding. Psyche is the breath of life, the animating force of our beings.

Eros and Psyche came together, a union of love and spirit, and birthed Pleasure. Pleasure is the symbolic and literal merging of a deep yearning (Eros) to express the human spirit (Psyche), our innate desire to be alive. Pleasure does not exist without love and a connection. Pleasure touches tastes, smells, sees, and listens with the depths of our hearts to our relationship to the earth. We enjoy the earth of our bodies and the land we live upon because Pleasure makes us feel the seamless connection of humanity and nature. A connection so inherently eternal and beautiful, that nourishes the heart and soul.

But what happened? Why is something as beautiful and life-giving as Pleasure feared and shunned? How is pleasure anything but enjoyable and satisfying? Why is guilt inextricably linked to pleasure for many people? Why is Pleasure considered forbidden, selfish, something we are unworthy of and must deny ourselves?

We turned the medicine of our human existence into a poison.

Pleasure Feast and Famine

We sat in a circle, myself and 30 women in my workshop, "The Art of Sensual Intelligence: Awakening Pleasure and Intimacy." I asked them a simple question: What is pleasure? Their answers are why I do this work.

Pleasure is:

Elusive.
Too vulnerable.
Performative. Not authentic.
A lot of cognitive energy. We have to battle to make space to feel true pleasure.
Difficult because we do not have a safe space.
Like a child just enjoying life now, so we cannot have pleasure. There is no time. There are things that we want to achieve.
Not natural to us.

Some of us have been shamed for feeling uninhibited pleasure. Some of us have shamed others for showing pleasure. We can get weird when we see others living fully and shamelessly enjoying themselves. Maybe they're licking their fingers in public, laughing or moaning just a little too loud for propriety. Maybe they just look too damned happy, and we kind of want to squash them and make them shut up, and tone it down.

Yes, that is the dark side of our relationship with pleasure. That visceral feeling in your body when you see or feel something beautiful, sensual, or erotic comes because we have been trained out of being comfortable with sensuality. We are taught to see pleasure as a threat, and humans tend to destroy threats.

But we're wired for pleasure. When we constantly deny ourselves this life nutrient, we end up creating a feast-or-famine relationship. We turn to compulsive, hedonistic binges; or we stay in denial and suppression. This erratic imbalance with ourselves warps our sense of pleasure so that we do not even know what it is for ourselves anymore. Yet, all hope is not lost. We are able to restore a healthy balance with pleasure when we embody the principles of pleasure: "slow down and savor."

Pleasure Gluttony

Hunger

I am hungry.
I am hungry both in my mind and in my body.
I want you
To fill my mind
To fill my body
With pleasures and ecstasy
With that beautiful lopsided smile and
Those eyes that should not have seen so much
And still have brilliant innocence
That glitters from their dark brown depths.
I wish you could want me as I want you.
I am ripened like the fallen fruit of the persimmon tree
Pick me cause I am ready,
Flesh melted to a clean sweet pudding to
Slurp in.
You usurp my concentration,
My logic
Cause I know this is not good for me
And yet
You still feel so fucking good.

You speak to that deep basic part of me that
Wants to be claimed hard and
Brought to my knees
As my ego dies and
Curls up into a little ball at your feet
So you can
Come down and pick me up and
Press me into your mouth
And masticate me with your power.

> *Chew me up,*
> *Your saliva pulling me up even tighter,*
> *Pulling me apart*
> *Dripping into me,*
> *Changing my cells,*
> *Changing my name*
> *Making me breaking me*
> *Into the wild primal radiant creature that I forgot I was.*
>
> View this poem in dance form:
> https://www.youtube.com/watch?v=a7PLgJNCJ2E

Benjamin was a Sensualist SQ type and prided himself on rocking women's worlds with orgasms. He was a good-looking man who loved to party and the pleasures of life. Not only did he love sex, but he also felt empowered by his ability to pay attention and bring erotic satisfaction to his lovers. But he felt empty. He said he was mainly used for his ability to give orgasms and for his good looks, but not for who he was. He struggled with really feeling who he was and desired more from life than just parties and fucking. He was stuck on this cycle of seeking and consuming pleasure, with no satiation in sight. He wanted to feel closeness, depth, and substance, but he couldn't figure out how.

Pleasure obsessors turn their pleasure outward and sometimes use it to keep things from getting too close and intimate. They try to disguise their suffering with adventures that oversaturate the senses. However, they often still feel bereft because the Pleasure "climax" is only a fleeting respite from pain and loneliness.

We will mistakenly think that love and relationship addiction, porn addiction, cheating, over-eating, and dependence on drugs and alcohol are indulging in pleasure. Having no impulse control and no qualms about doing whatever our primal urges tell us is not pleasure. It is compulsive reactivity. These are signs that a deeper need is not being met. That need is to honor and listen to the intelligence of pleasure consistently. Because we were not trained to form a clear relationship with our Pleasure and desire, we can struggle to see the signs of when we are Pleasure starved.

The poem "Hunger" is a response when I encountered the depths of desire without the depths of heart connection. It is absolutely delicious, propelling, because Eros is pure inspiration and is an honorable and intelligent pursuit. However, the full potency of Pleasure in the interplay of Eros (desire and masculine energy) and Psyche (spirit, heart, and feminine energy. When the ratio of Eros to Psyche is imbalanced toward Eros, we will still feel hungry. This is because Eros is pure desire, and to desire is to want more. While Eros is an incredible force that gets us moving, we have to slow down and stop in order to receive that for which we are striving.

When we chase pleasure, we put our bodies in a stressed, sympathetic state. The act of chasing is an embodiment of scarcity and fear. This embodied mechanism turns on the impulse to keep pushing us to go for more, more sensation, and faster.

Retraining Pleasure gluttony is to reconnect with the soft part of Pleasure, Pleasure's mother, Psyche. Psyche is the human spirit, our soul. When we honor the desire of the human spirit, then we open ourselves to have a loving relationship with our bodies, a relationship in which we seek the soul's growth through the body. Psyche offers a grounding, sustaining force.

We do this by following Pleasure's motto: Slow down and savor. Slowing down engages the parasympathetic nervous system, which allows us to relax and feel full. Focus on enjoyment and appreciation. Allow the experience to keep unfolding within.

> ### SIP
> ### How to Slow Down
>
> 1. When has your need for pleasure just taken over you?
> 2. What happened?
> 3. How did you feel afterward?
>
> The next time you feel your Pleasure desire pulling you in a direction that may not lead to your ultimate desired outcome, ask yourself:
>
> 4. What is it that I am *really* wanting?
> 5. What does my Eros (desire) want?
> 6. What does my Psyche (soul and heart) want?
> 7. Is there a way I can satisfy both?

Pleasure Suppression

Rebecca was a "good girl," a Domme SQ type. Her mother taught her to cross her legs and act like a "proper young lady." She was a dancer growing up, and while she loved it, the strict nature of her ballet training focused on perfect lines and execution rather than exploring artistic expression.

Her corporate job was demanding, and she wore her hair in tight, controlled buns reminiscent of her ballet days. She came to my "Unleash Your Diva" workshop because she felt stuck in her life, in her relationships, and disconnected from her body. She hadn't felt joy and aliveness in a very long time, and the judging voice of her mother, plus the strict, regimented rules she grew up in, wrecked her ability to engage in intimacy. She would get stuck in her head and couldn't stop thinking about work. It didn't help that she *hated* her job and felt that the people on her team were sabotaging her when she spoke up.

Aka, she was freaking miserable.

Rebecca's story is very common. The "good girl" can be successful and desired because she operates within the rules (patriarchy) that demand that she suppress her truth and desires if she wants to be respected. To be the perfect amount of outspoken and cute, but not too much, lest she get labeled a bitch or a slut, she has to carefully choreograph her actions. In the process, she completely loses touch with herself and has shut down her connection to pleasure.

In the pursuit of productivity, the value of humanity, sustainability, and regeneration got lost. We were taught that discomfort is good and leads to success. In school, we sat in rows under fluorescent lights. As adults, we sit in cubicles under fluorescent lights. Professionality looks like neckties tied as tight as nooses; hot suit jackets are worn even in the heat of summer; high-heeled shoes pinch the feet and cut off circulation; skirts and other clothing hinder the movement of the body, creating lines and angles of uniformed order, color, and shape.

The biggest irony is that people who suppress Pleasure often come to believe that they do not deserve Pleasure, or that somehow, Pleasure is dangerous. This message becomes internalized to the point that they cannot see or accept pleasure when it comes their way. Pleasure, like all of the other 7Ps of Sensual Expression, has intelligence. If we suppress that intelligence, then we disconnect from body, mind, and heart. When we disconnect from Pleasure there is an energy of sadness, insecurity, anger, and/or feeling lost. We deny the fecundity of feeling lush delights, magnificent, beautiful; when we suppress pleasure, it turns toxic and consumes us from the inside.

My mother is a social worker, which, along with many careers in the social, human services (including, but not limited to nursing, policing, etc.), has an alarming rate of cancer, heart disease, and depression. Stress is a silent killer, resulting from the mind, heart, and body attempting to cope with the concentration of seeing the worst of humanity. In order to survive their job, they often deny their own health and wellbeing.

We have to slowly give ourselves the nourishment we so desperately need. Connecting with pleasure allows us to open up to the gift of receiving, knowing our boundaries, opening up to feel in our bodies.

When we do this we realize we are soft and sensitive—some people have never had that experience of themselves before. There's no shame in being soft and sensitive. We are tough and strong, but these are traits that are forced upon us instead of things that we really feel.

Patriarchy and colonialism will tell us that we have to push ourselves so hard that we break, that we burn out. It tells us to constantly delay gratification, ignore the wisdom of our bodies and our senses so that we can be productive machines that do not feel. It has said, through history and culture, implicitly and explicitly, that your body is not yours, not yours to explore, celebrate, adorn, and behold. And then we believe that in order to receive love we have to give so much of ourselves away that we don't even know ourselves.

This is not the way.

It is time to create a relationship with ourselves. Creating a healthy relationship with pleasure is about taking ownership of your body.

I worked with Rebecca for over a year, both in one-on-one work and in group programs, and this was her journey: learning to reclaim and express her human spirit, her heart, her yearning through pleasure. This was different from her previous modus operandi of "I have to work in this way, look this way, treat myself this way in order to produce this result."

Instead, she learned that she was *more* effective through the Pleasure of her body. Her deep-rooted pleasure was a compass of her health and well-being. She got to feel herself being a contribution to the world. How her work could be nourishing and filling up her cup.

When she did this, her whole demeanor shifted. Pleasure entered her body, her heart, and mind, and she became more creative. She allowed herself to create dances that were expressive, rather than focused on strict technique. She brought her expressive dance to a company creativity fundraiser, and it was an expression of *her*, a part of her that no one on her team had experienced because she was so busy keeping everything controlled and correct. She learned to laugh at herself and with herself when she noticed her perfectionist habits were pushing away the romantic possibility she was interested in.

It's funny how much being reminded to take that ballet bun out of your hair and get a cute, flirty, layered haircut can tell your mind that Pleasure is safe. Or how taking off toe-pinching shoes and walking in the grass barefoot reminds you that your every step is a gift to be savored. Consider how doing a weird dance move instead of the perfect dance move gets you back in your body, and connected to your Pleasure.

What are you missing out on when you're being prim and proper instead of exploring the juicy readiness of life in your body?

SIP
Healing Repressed Pleasure

Pay attention to the messages you tell yourself about pleasure.
1. Whose messages are these?
2. Is this the wisdom of your body, of pleasure, or is a disconnective narrative dictating you?

Take note where you feel self-conscious, or resistant to Pleasure.
3. What do you do to resist or block pleasure?

After you write it down, turn on music that reflects how you feel when you are resisting Pleasure and let it flow through and out of your body.

> 4. What can you do to allow more pleasure into your life?
>
> Now turn on a song that inspires pleasure and enjoyment of yourself. Move, stretch, luxuriate, take up space, and make sounds to vibrate your body with Pleasure.
>
> You've got this!

Creating a Healthy Relationship with Pleasure

It doesn't matter what side of the spectrum we may fall on, the key is feeding ourselves enough pleasure on a daily basis. You can always go slower, you can always pay more attention, you can always feel more deeply. Reconnect to our bodies and the rhythm of the earth. You fill up your cup—your body vessel—with love, spirit, and connection.

Pleasure is all about slowing down and allowing your being to be pulled and seduced by the present moment. This is the dance of Eros and Psyche, movement and receptivity. This slowing down is to allow yourself to be present, to sit with each moment and savor the miracle of it. Pleasure comes not in the absence of pain, but through our willingness to also sit with it, through it, knowing that to experience sunshine, we must feel the joy of rain; to understand the light, we must connect to the beauty of the dark. To feel the depths of Pleasure, we must delve into the beautiful lessons of pain.

Connecting and accepting pleasure is also a connection to intuition, creating full sensual engagement inside our bodies. When we are engaged, we are in the full flavor of the experience.

SIP
Embody Pleasure

Pleasure is a whole meal, not just dessert.

A lot of times we get caught up in the "I don't have enough time to slow down" mindset. Pleasure is the last thing on your mind because you have so much to do, or you're just not in the mood. Most of us wait to indulge in Pleasure when we finally get home from work, or when we finally go on that vacation, or when we finally retire. However, Pleasure is like food: if you don't eat you starve. If you wait too long to eat, your body will eat itself. If you eat too much, then you can make yourself sick.

Do not wait to reward yourself with Pleasure. It's not a one-time thing. Instead, make Pleasure your daily meal because it is a necessary nutrient of life.

Try this exercise to embody the richness and wisdom of Pleasure.

Say the word "Pleasure" out loud.
Pleasure.

Explore the feel and sound of the word as the idea lights up in your brain, and you use your breath, vocal cords, and mouth to say the word "Pleasure.
Let the "P" press your lips together and then pop them open. Aspirate the letter "P" with deep breaths.
Flick the letter "l" your tongue against your teeth.
Say "Pl" all together and feel the staccato movement.
Allow your jaw to soften as you aspirate the "ea" vowels. Try drawing out the vowel sound by widening your mouth and letting the sound be a moan.
The "s" pulls a cool shushing, a whispered purr quieting your heart.
"Ur" urges your mouth to kiss the end of the word with languid urgency.
Be in the silence of the last "e."
Sit with yourself and just be with the experience of the word Pleasure.

This exercise, though short and simple, is multi-layered in its benefits:

1. We use our mouths, lips, tongues and teeth to roll the word around in our mouths. This allows us to experience the word Pleasure like we would our food.

2. We are forced to slow down and savor ourselves.

3. When we repeat and put attention on a word or a concept

4. We are using embodiment to reinforce and train the experience of pleasure so that we experience the concept both cognitively (IQ) as well as sensually and kinesthetically (SQ). The resulting emotional experience of doing this exercise also stimulates EQ.

Chapter 17 Summary

- Pleasure is delight and desire.
- It is about savoring the moment and taking your time.
- Pleasure is not about only chasing the sweetness.
- Suppressed pleasure does not make it disappear. If that suppressed pleasure leaks outward, we will gorge our starving senses on whatever feels good at the moment, even if it ultimately hurts us.
- Fill yourself up with bodily delights, because pleasure is the whole meal, not just dessert.

Chapter 18

PLAY –
THE JOURNEY OF CURIOSITY AND EXPLORATION

Black Mermaid

A dark sinewy body. A black shadow under the depths. Her hair flows in spiraled, kinky coils, trapping air bubbles that rise and pop, swirling tornadoes of underwater wind that make the dolphins swing, giggle, and spin.

She is the whirlpool, the pull of the waves, the joy and play of the oceans.

A black mermaid, the curls of her hair dancing, teasing, giving life to all those around. Live, play, explore, spread joy, be free.

Element: Air

Characteristics: Light-hearted, fun, childlike, visionary.

Associated SQ Type: The Creative

Embodied Sound: Eeee!

Embodied Gesture: A frolicking leap! Throwing arms up and head back cheerfully.

Motto: I create joy, lightness, and laughter in any situation.

Embodiment (Body)	**Body Language**: Can be body or mind prominent. Light on their feet. Quick and adaptive body movements. Quick, aspirated sounds like squeals, playful shouts, and fast breath from excitement.
	Balanced: Joyful, inviting, energetic, and open, a breath of fresh air, effervescent, bouncy, ready to play, ready smile. Hair twirling, light, and musical voice and movement.
	Unbalanced: Restless, and fidgeting. Not grounded, flighty. Can poke fun at, sardonic and ironic about the body, so can neglect or poke fun at the body. Difficulty being still and calm in the body.
Self-Love (Heart)	**Balanced**: Joyful, effervescent, happy, inviting, innocence and simplicity. Enthusiastic.
	Unbalanced: Immature, petty, throws temper tantrums, impulsive, self-deprecating, bratty. Uses play, jokes, games, silliness, and not taking things seriously to distract from difficult emotions. Difficulty staying in the present moment with stillness.
Mindfulness (Mind)	"How do I make this fun?"
	Balanced: Childlike wonder. Fresh and new eyes. An innovative, adaptable, witty, and quick thinker.
	Unbalanced: Disconnected from reality, scattered, unreliable, flakey, scheming, always joking.

Community	**Balanced**: Life of the party. Brings the trickster energy, counter-culture. Points out and plays with the absurd, the overlooked connections. Uses humor and fun to unearth buried truths. Artistic and visionary.
	Unbalanced: Bitter and mean-spirited dark comedy. Disconnects by poking holes through connections. Divisive trickster. Unreliable, flighty, judging the heaviness of the world while keeping separate from it.

Play is the inner child. Aliveness, embodiment, and sensual exploration are possible because of Play. Play is permission, curiosity, levity, and an invitation to share that which gives us joy. It is one of the most underrated of the 7Ps. However, we learn to confine play to childhood or maybe dust it off and use it when we have kids. It's simply not cool to be genuinely earnest. It's best to appear worldly and jaded, like we know it all, been there, done that.

Play unlocks laughter by opening us to our imagination and creative possibilities. Laughter is the antidote to disconnection and stagnance because when the brain laughs, our guard comes down. Endorphins flood our systems, washing our internal organs with the message to relax and be present in our bodies. Play speaks directly to the lightness of spirit and expression of the heart. It is a crucial component to creating connection and community because it breaks down our defenses and makes a common focal point of joy.

You Play Too Much!

OK, here's a riddle for you!

What is fluent in sarcasm, does not take things too seriously, is a staunch believer in "no drama, please," and has a severe allergy to adulting?

Someone in the modern online dating scene? That's your guess?

That's not the answer, but it's very close.

In truth, the modern dating scene and these characteristics all have the same root: imbalanced Play.

Play brings the energy of the inner child. It is curious, engaging, whimsical. Yet, taken to extremes, this does make a person unreliable, insensitive, and flighty.

Jaime was a Creative SQ Type. She loved her dance classes, and her calendar was always full of fun activities. She studied design in college and was a Jill of all trades. By the time we met, Jaime was working as an event coordinator and was constantly on the go. She was skilled at connecting people and organizations with her contagiously bubbly attitude, making her a natural at her job.

However, as happy-go-lucky as Jaime was, she came to my workshops and said, "I only know how to be silly, not sensual. I feel weird when I am sensual." Jaime didn't know how to connect in a way that did not involve being silly, and her intimate relationships were suffering. She had tried going to sensual dance classes to help bring out her "hotness," but she was still acting and playing when she danced. Jaime could not own the sexy body movements because they didn't feel natural. The only way she could do it was through playing games.

During a session, I invited Jaime to take a deep breath down to her belly, slowly breathe out, and feel into her heart and her body. Then I asked her, "What are you running away from? What keeps you constantly moving so much that you cannot sit still and be with yourself?" Her body fidgeted as she told me that her parents had high expectations of her, and these expectations did not align with who she was. However, she did not feel safe being herself and showing her real feelings. Instead, she would always show her sunny side so that her parents wouldn't be disappointed. She made sure everyone around her was happy.

Play's element is air, so, at its extremes, interactions become fraught with dizzying energy. Jaime became frantic, using Play to deflect perceived threats. Constant joking, sarcasm, witty remarks, and cute girlish giggling became defense mechanisms that averted her parents' criticism but ultimately created distance rather than connection.

When we cannot balance Play, we lose the ability to connect with the genuine expression of our bodies and grounded sensual needs. There was never a dull moment for Jaime, but there was never any time for her to be grounded and still enough for genuine reflection and relatedness, both to herself and others. Over-dependence on Play kept her from getting the intimacy and potency she craved from herself and her intimate partnerships.

For Jaime, the road to returning to her body and balancing out her Play energy involved going on the Journey of Peace (Chapter 23) and *then* Pleasure (Chapter 17). Though Jaime expressed a desire for Peace's qualities of nurturance and nourishment would allow her to find safety in slowing down and feeling her emotions. Only then would she be ready to explore Pleasure, because Pleasure requires a more profound stillness and a concentrated savoring, which was the exact opposite of how she had learned to be in the world.

It was not easy for Jaime to bring gentle, loving awareness and acceptance to her body and emotional expression. She dodged her power nearly her whole life. But, with continued practice, she started to *embody* feeling safety with herself rather than bounding away from her genuine expression.

SIP
Balancing Play

If you are someone for whom Play is significant in your life, and it feels challenging to stay connected to your body without making light of the situation or yourself, try out what I did with Jaime.

The first step is to bring awareness to your body. Start with asking yourself when and where you tend to feel the desire to squirm or wiggle your way through something.

Pay attention to it. Breathe with it and notice the sensations in your body.

Ask yourself: What is it that you need? What are you trying to tell me?

Breathe again and listen.

Look at the characteristics of each of the 7Ps. See which one most closely matches what your heart and body told you. For example, do you need Peace, like Jaime? Or maybe your body is asking for Power, Passion, or Philosophy.

All Work, No Play

Some people, especially doctors, lawyers, therapists, and corporate folks, admit that they have lost play, freedom, and joy in their lives. To "survive" and thrive in their job, they had to give up that part of themselves.

Salina was a doctor, self-made, and driven (SQ Type Domme). The words "stop, slow down, relax, ask for help" were not in her vocabulary. She regularly drove herself to the brink, constantly proving that she was capable, and she had no sympathy for those who did not also push themselves. When she decided to open her first medical practice (a giant undertaking in and of itself), not only did she do this while she was pregnant, she also had a toddler, and her father was dying. While she "succeeded," Salina's health deteriorated to the point of total burnout, and her intimate relationship practically did not exist.

She came to me after I led an embodiment workshop for entrepreneurs, and everyone was laughing, opening up, connecting, and networking sweetly and easily. Her business and relationships struggled because she had trouble bonding with people beyond transactional interactions. (Transactional relationships occur not just via money but also in favors and tit-for-tat in her intimate relationships.) She wanted to take her entrepreneurship to the next level and realized that connection was just as, if not more so, essential to success in her career as was her extensive training and expertise.

"I want to get back into my body and connect with my softness and femininity," she told me.

Salina's body language was stilted and stiff. She was a beautiful woman, in her 50s and in incredible shape. Yet, there was no life in her voice, no energy in her body. Her entire embodiment was that of "all work and no play."

What Salina needed was a reboot and a reintroduction to the parts of herself that she had been pressing down ever since she was a child, trying to prove herself to her father.

I suggested starting with a day-long session with Salina in the forest. It was out of her comfort zone but still comfortable, with no distractions and no one for whom she had to perform. I found a secret spot and laid out some goodies on the ground for her to discover. I wanted it to look like the wood nymphs had come and made a special place for her.

I let her lead us through the forest. When we came to the path leading to the secret spot I'd set up, I said conspiratorially, "Ooo! That path looks interesting! Let's explore there!"

She gave a small chuckle and led the way, stopping when she found the spot.

"Oh, look," she said, pointing at the ground. "Someone left these here."

"Let's check it out!"

There we found a rose quartz crystal set on her favorite color silk scarf, ylang-ylang essential oil for balance, and a handbound journal, all framed by nearby sticks and leaves. The wood fairies had come!

Her face wavered back and forth between a small, slightly chagrined smile and an all-out cheese-eating grin. So cute!

We sat down cross-legged, two grown, professional women on the search to find joy, aliveness, and connection. Like many prestigious professionals, she learned to push down her feelings and present a professional, controlled front. What is not taught is that this suppression training has actual health, relationship, and career consequences that hurt in the long run.

We had to go on a journey to reclaim what brought her to life. Though her initial focus was her career, one of the benefits of finding your Sensual Intelligence in one area of your life is that it starts to affect other parts of your life as well. The Sensual Intelligence journey is holistic. Each element influences the whole.

I asked her about her childhood, and she told me about that time she skinned her knee because she was so competitive. I asked her to teach me some of the songs, dances, and games she used to play with her friends. Salina was on the journey to remember, reclaim and embody her Play, light-heartedness, and joy she had before she became a dour medical professional.

She taught me her version of Ms. Mary Mac. I one-upped her with some "Down-down baby, down by the roller coaster," and soon we were sassily rolling our hips and singing, "Let's get the rhythm of the hot dog." She one-upped me again by showing me a jump-rope song and dance I had never seen before.

We laughed and listened to the birds in the trees laughing with us. We put hands and feet to the earth, we sang, and we thanked the ancestors for everything they went through that allowed us to play. She told me she had not laughed and played like that since childhood. She was glowing.

Salina, like many of us in our drive to achieve our goals, had forgotten the value of play, real, goofy, ungraceful Play, as a part of life. It brings joy, happiness, and a sense of fulfillment that "success," getting the job done, and being at the top cannot give. Play is the connection creator and permission granter. There's nothing like the joyful spaciousness that comes after we tickle the rules of life.

SIP
Tickle Your Life

Journal

When was the last time you shut down your inner child?

What would your inner child have done if you could do it over?

Activity

Play opens us, opens our minds, and the creative centers in our body. From a neuroplasticity perspective, play creates a space for curiosity and safety for us to explore.

Bring a lightness to the exploration and curiosity of your own body.

When we bring that light, playful exploration to embodiment and sensuality, this can shift our relationship to ourselves, to our pleasure, so that it is not goal-oriented. Instead, it is journey-oriented.

Here are some things to do to tickle your life with more play!

1. Set the container: This is a safe enough space for us to explore being: silly, awkward, funny, exaggerated
2. Exaggerate everything: too big, too small, too loud, too soft
3. When there's a mistake, make a pact to celebrate it
4. Bouncy anything is a good thing
5. Costumes and toys, stuffed animals, and anything that reminds you of childhood
6. Pillow fights, wrestling, tickling, play-acting

The Healing Power of Play

The biggest thing missing in most of our lives is Play. We're so serious! I always have silliness and play in my teachings. For a while, I worked as an MC for conferences and events. I called myself a "conference catalyst" because I facilitated connections amongst participants. I would get everyone moving and engaging with each other using a variety of activities, all based on the principles of Sensual Intelligence.

At one of these conferences, a man in his 50s made his way through the crowd of 300 conference participants. With his face bright and shining, he approached me and said, "My wife has been trying to get me to dance for years, and I never could do it. I love her, but the dancing feels awkward. But, after the first day of the conference, I went home and danced with my wife for the first time! I even dipped her! She was ecstatic! And I want to thank you because I never felt permission to be playful. It's been so liberating! Thank you."

I've experienced something not talked about enough: men are discouraged from exploring anything but being stiffly masculine, stoic, and in charge. The same gender stereotypes that say women should be pretty and docile tell men not to be silly and shake their booties. This severely limits the scope of expression and rapport. Play offers a structure in which everyone can explore themselves, their bodies, and their expression without fear of "losing face" or status. Theater, acting, charades, and Sensual Intelligence, offer an opportunity to explore outside of the box of proper masculinity.

From ice-breakers to foreplay, the gift of play is endearing and unguarded authenticity that is contagious. It has the power to transform shame and embarrassment into humor and relatability through shared absurdity. We get to look behind the veil at all the arbitrary rules and conditioning we bind ourselves with, and those glimpses show us just how constructed and malleable our lives are. We see that we have a choice with how we engage with life, the world, and our circumstances. Our brains literally cannot judge and be inhibited at the same time as we are open and laughing.

And yes, you have permission to make that silly face! I double dare you!

Chapter 18 Summary

- Play is permission, curiosity, levity, and an invitation to share that which gives us joy.
- Play is a key component to creating connection and community because it breaks down our guard and defenses.
- Play has the power to transform shame and embarrassment into humor and relatability through shared absurdity.
- We balance Play by being open to curiosity and wonder yet still centered in ourselves and our inner knowing.

Chapter 19

Passion –
The Journey of the Fire of the Heart

Passion

You teach me to break open,
To split my ego down the middle and spill it
Onto the deep dark earth.
And the earth opens her legs wide and allows me to enter her body,
Mixing with the blood of her soil, and her love,
And she births PASSION.

Passion is pain and pleasure,
Experiences of suffering, mistakes, and crimes against our own souls
Made beautiful

I own the passion of my heart.
I have earned it.

Element: Fire

Characteristics: Emotive, Catalyzing, Untamed, Free, Expressive

Associated SQ Type: The Diva

Embodied Voice: Guttural, low-belly "Rawr!"

Embodied Gestures: Wide-legged foot stomp, thigh slap, and quick, wild arms.

Motto: I am fearless, fierce, and free. I tend to the fire of my heart.

Embodiment (Body)	**Body Language:** No filter between emotions and body language. Clear mind-body connection Emotions are worn on their sleeve. **Balanced:** Uses body fully to move the space, big gestures, emphatic, rousing. Big voice, warm hugs, welcoming and invigorating. **Unbalanced:** Dramatic, destructive, careless in their expression. Can physically overpower using physical size and volume, can throw temper tantrums.
Self-Love (Heart)	**Balanced:** Free, expressive, wild, clear, and bright emotions. Big-hearted and loving. **Unbalanced:** Lashes out, is destructive, and unaware of the consequences of big emotions. Can be victimized. Indulge in anger, betrayal. Difficulty feeling vulnerability and softness.
Mindfulness (Mind)	**Balanced:** "How can I bring aliveness, intensity, and depth?" Able to engage intense and charged emotions to create clarity of mind. **Unbalanced:** "Everyone is against me or out to get me." Rush to conclusions, irrational, erratic, destructive thinking.

Community	**Balanced**: Brings life, warmth, vitality, and depth in all things. Refreshing in their honesty. Inspires community to rise together under a cause. Sempiira. The champion, hero, or cheerleader.
	Unbalanced: The "bitch" or the "asshole". Firestarter and instigator of drama. Wildly inconsiderate. Creates chaos.

Fire illuminates, warms, and clarifies. When it is out of control, it burns and destroys. Without fire, things become stagnant, dark, and diseased. The same is true for the intelligence of Passion.

In Sensual Intelligence, Passion is the big moving energy that can galvanize people to move with conviction. It lights the burning flame of our heart and sets our boundaries by illuminating the truth of our "hell yes" and our "fuck no." In intimate relationships, passion is the sexy, primal, carnal, and erotic bliss. The wisdom of passion is wild, free, and expressive.

People feel nostalgia for their childhood because they were uninhibited. Children on the playground are the embodiment of Passion. They scream at the top of their lungs, rip their clothes, and have wild, crazy hair. Life erupts through their bodies as they freely take up space and are present and full of life. They don't care that they look like hot shit; they're *alive!* Kids go through the full gamut of emotions: joy, exuberance, rage, anger, grief, sorrow, arousal, and excitement. They immerse themselves in intense emotions, unintimidated by shame or judgment of what they may feel or why.

The history of the word passion perfectly reflects the complexity of how we relate to it. Passion originally meant "to endure pain and suffering." In Christianity, Jesus's crucifixion is also called "the passion of the Christ." It is said that the crucifixion was an act of love despite the pain he endured (and perhaps because of the pain). I think this explains our strange, strange love-hate relationship with pain and Passion.

Pain is not inherently bad. It helps us establish our body's boundaries. You put your hand in a fire and... ouch! Pain. You learn not to put your hand in a fire.

This goes for the boundaries of the heart as well. When we do not follow our passion, we will know pain, the pain that comes from not following the joy of our hearts.

Additionally, when we are truly passionate about something (or someone), we are pushed along by our desire to the point where we are willing to endure pain, suffering, and loss for it. No pain, no gain, right? The modern definition of passion carries a complex force that often compels us to do things, even at our own demise.

It is no wonder passion makes us scared and crazy! It is the ultimate moving force, and we are simply not accustomed to letting our hearts move! We want to control ourselves and be predictable so our feelings don't overrun us. But when we avoid or try to "clean up" Passion, we make ourselves fall victim to its whims. We end up having a reactive instead of proactive relationship with Passion.

There is nothing wrong with Passion, it's just that in this society, buttoning up your shirt to your neck and wearing a tie as tight as a noose are signs of power and control. Movement, dance, joy, passion, are signs of wild, uncontrollable urges, which threaten the order of society. So we end up pushing everything down or letting ourselves flare out of control.

Wild Passion

Felicity regularly had temper tantrums. She hit other students, ignored practically all instructions, and had a lot of attitude. She had experienced more violence and trauma in her life than most people's darkest nightmares, but so had all of the other students and the staff. They had all lived through a war. Everyone deals with trauma differently, and Felicity chose rage.

Felicity had been taught all of the right tools for emotional regulation: meditation, yoga, breathwork, you name it. Whenever she acted out, every teacher told her some version of "just breathe through your anger," or "meditate to calm yourself down." But, of course, this would make her even more livid and frustrated.

Yes, breathing, meditation, and mindfulness are amazing tools for healing, but that's not how these tools were being used. Felicity was actually being told to push down her feelings and act like a good girl; meditate herself to decency, and breathe to be quiet and get in line. I know this because I also did this to her. All I wanted was peace, quiet, and ease, and Felicity's outbursts made my job more difficult. It was convenient for me to tell her to meditate, then blame and lecture her had another outburst. My thinking was, "You can take a horse to water, but you can't make it drink." I put the onus on Felicity.

Then, one night at bedtime, after a particularly trying day with Felicity, there was a terrifying electrical storm. The sky turned a greenish-black, lightning ripped the sky, thunder shook the bed, and rain drowned out the sound of the world. That night, as strange as it may sound, I swear the spirit of Felicity's mom visited my dreams.

Her mother told me that my job was to help her daughter heal and that I was not doing that. She said that I was putting on the facade of helping and not actually putting in the work. I argued with her and denied it, but deep down, I knew she was right. So I promised Felicity's mom that I would open my heart to her, look beyond her acerbic temperament, and do what I was supposed to do: help Felicity.

The next day, I grabbed two pillows and invited Felicity to join me in a private room. I tossed the pillow and told her to hit me with it. "Come on! Let's have a pillow fight!" I gently tapped her with the pillow. Felicity completely ignored me. "Come on! Use your pillow and hit me!" I tapped her more forcefully, but she just sat on the floor, stiff and despondent.

I swung my pillow at her again, goading and taunting. All of a sudden, she grunted, jumped to her feet, and launched at me, swinging her pillow with all her might. Her teeth were bared, and her breath came fast and harsh, bits of spittle flying with her efforts.

Letting her swing, I simply blocked her from hitting me in the face. Her swings got wilder and wilder, and sometimes the bones of our arms would hit with a jarring thud, but we kept on going. As she kept swinging and hitting, her grunts of effort turned into moans. Her moans turned into anguished heaves. Those anguished, chest-throbbing heaves turned into crying and sobbing. And then she was screaming as her tears flooded her dark brown cheeks. Finally, she fell to the floor, curled her body tightly around the pillow, while a tsunami of tears, screams, rage, anger, and grief poured out of her.

"I'm so angry that my mother left me! Why did she leave me!? I hate her for leaving me!" she raged between the sobs.

So *that* was what her mother's spirit was telling me the night when she visited my dreams. Felicity was angry that her mother had died and left her all alone. That was why she raged. Felicity had never been given the permission to grieve how she needed to grieve fully, so those emotions poisoned her from the inside, making her sometimes depressed and other times, aggressive.

Every aggressive deed, every act of defiance, was a little bit of grief slipping through her defenses. She had to reclaim her anger, her passion, and her emotions. She had to get to know them and embody them. She needed to feel their wisdom. After she was given permission and space to be in her truth about this abandonment, she could access her Peace.

After she finished crying, I asked her if she wanted a hug. She snuggled in my arms, and I held her. Between shaky breaths and small hiccups, she told me about her mother and her childhood before the accident. I asked her what she wanted to do next. She said she wanted to go for a walk and just be with herself.

She went to the ocean that day and walked for a long time. The salt of the ocean understood and the salt of her tears. From that day forward, Felicity never acted out again. She was able to regulate her emotions and use all of the breathing, yoga, and meditation techniques that everyone had been forcing down her throat.

She had been seen. She had been witnessed. Her emotions had space to express, and her existence was validated. Simple as that.

We must acknowledge and honor the process of our emotional passion. If we do not allow Passion to express itself, we do not learn how to safely and constructively wield it. When we do not listen to the wisdom of our passion, we will not know if we need to stoke our flames brighter so that the fire of our hearts doesn't sputter out. We will not be able to feel when our flames burn so bright that we even burn ourselves, burn others, and are consumed by our rage, anger, or jealousy.

We can only heal what we can feel and acknowledge. Anger and other big emotions indicate when we have violated our values. Having a relationship with all of our emotions gives us a choice in how we will be with them, as opposed to being taken over by them.

This is why I created the "Anger and Betrayal Healing Journey." This is meant to create a safe container for my clients to explore what parts they have held back, especially their raw, wild emotions. We need emotions to move our souls and our energy; otherwise, we become internally stagnant or destructive. I teach this and other Sensual Intelligence embodiment activities in my courses. It is important that when we go on these internal journeys to explore intense emotions, we do it in a safe, intentional container and to include aftercare meditation.

In the meantime, try out the activity I did with Felicity for yourself. Get a pillow, clear out anything breakable, and allow yourself the freedom to express yourself. The heat in your heart is passion. Let it be free.

Dampened Passion

I'm a recovering perfectionist.

I used my napkin perfectly. I stood up perfectly straight, and I always spoke properly (I've loosened up in my years because it weirded people out that I enunciated every word). I got perfect grades. I hid my imperfections and shied away from challenging situations where I might fall on my face. I had total meltdowns when I didn't do something perfectly: temper tantrums, crying, and ugly self-talk, that no one witnessed except for me.

On the outside, I was a good girl. I didn't have any needs. I could take care of myself. I could handle it. I could handle anything, all the stress, with poise, grace, and dignity, until that shit almost killed me. I literally held onto my shit, just as proper and quiet as I could be. Yet, I became anxious and constipated to the point where I poisoned the inside of my body. I ended up in a tiny clinic in el campo of Venezuela, on a questionable toilet, with an IV punctured through my arm, screaming for my mother. I had been too proud to ask for help, too arrogant to be seen as "failing," too proper to get ugly and passionate. I paid the price.

Passion gets a bad reputation because of how big it can make us. What if we move in a way that makes us unacceptable or too much for our restrained society? What if we're seen as messy, unprofessional, or weak? Women, especially, are either scared or fed up with being called a bitch, too much, out there, the "angry Black woman", the "dragon Asian lady", the "spicy Latina", while stoicism, emotional reserve, and coldness are acceptable and lauded. We've been told to restrict our bodies because that is what is needed to be a woman.

Perfection and propriety are killing us. For those who manage to "keep it together" on the outside, we tend to implode in sickness, adrenal fatigue, and hypertension, all for the sake of appearing prim and proper.

Perfection, the cold stoic, are all fake. These are the tools of the patriarchy that are meant to control who we are, and it's making us sick, unskilled, and irresponsible. Since we fear and avoid Passion, we lose connection to the power of our internal fire, and when we lose connection to it, we do not know how to wield it constructively. We end up either dousing our fires and then having unpredictable outbursts or exploding in fits of rage. This is because we do not have an active, alive, and integrated relationship with our Passion.

How do you have Sensually Intelligent Passion?

One of the biggest fears around passion is "losing control." People are afraid that they will lose control and destroy life if they follow their passion. True control is not simply putting something in a neat and constrictive box. Control is when you can dial up or down your emotional experience in a safe, authentic way. You have to be intimately connected to yourself and your expression to do this. With SQ, control is deep intimacy with your body and its *expression*, not its suppression. If you are suppressing and caging something in, it means that it is out of control.

We build a relationship with our Passion by stoking our own inner flame: our *sempiira*. This is when we move the energy of passion and direct our fire.

Sempiira is a Ugandan word meaning "a fire that is built for constructive purposes."[20] When we have a conscious relationship with Passion it becomes a constructive force in our lives. Use the tools of Sensual IQ to transform the raw fire of Passion into a *sempiira*.

Passionate Woman

Embody the energy of initiative & push through your own limitations.
Warrior woman
Wild woman
Feminine fire,
Heathen release and embodied celebration of movement,
Our life's blood,
Deep guttural sounds of ecstasy,
The power of intention
You are the fire lit from within.

---

[20] Askhari Johnson Hodari, Ph.D. *The African Book of Names*.
http://www.hcibooks.com/pressreleasepdf/9780757307799.pdf

Movement is the medicine that unleashes the ardent, bristling creature inside you: an incandescent ferocity and palpable courage. When done right, Passion can be the *sempiira* of your heart. So let us build a fire in your life: gathering the fodder, lighting the flint, feeling the first lick of the flames, being totally engulfed in the first, allowing ourselves and our environment to be illuminated by the light of the flames, and finally, after all the excess as been burned down, we are left with the beautiful, pure, essence of *you*.

To gather the fodder, you must own all of the emotions you have been denying yourself. You will know which ones they are by what brings your heart a bit of fear. Look into any areas of anger, jealousy, desire, arousal: this is your passion story.

Lighting the flint is putting your passion story out into the world. Breathe in and feel the energy of the emotion, fill your chest, and let that warmth fill your entire body. Take your passion story from your thoughts and memories and write it down. Then use your voice and tell your story out loud. Even better is if you can share it in Community, be that one trusted person, trusted group, or even an old tree. Share it and be witnessed.

You will feel the first lick of flames when you allow yourself to go from a simple telling of the story to an embodied enactment of the story. Turn on music that can be an audio soundscape, fanning the flames of your truth. Let your passion story move through your body, starting from the center of your chest and radiating out your limbs. Get in front of the drums, paint, or any instrument that lets your original primal body express. You are an ancient queen, king, primordial being. You deserve to never feel constrained. The passion in your voice does not even have to have words; it may reduce down to its pure essence of sound and motion. Let your body dance and let the story transform and take flight through you.

Get down on your hands and knees. Growl, yell, and gyrate your hips so that you connect to the primal, wild parts of your body. Let go of the words and simply allow the movement of consonants and vowels. As you move, pull, grab, palpate, smack, kneed your own skin. Thoroughly explore the motion of your skin, muscles, and bones of your being. Let the magic of being in your body be the healing. Step out of your head and be present. This is what feeling free and wild is. It is time to come to life.

Move, sound, breathe until you are empty, complete, burned clean and clarified, baptized in the flames of your fire. Lay down on your back, heart open, hands to your sides, or curled up in a ball on your side, holding yourself. You are wild. You are passionate. You are uncontrolled and unrestrained, especially in pursuit of pleasure. Allow yourself to live or grow in the natural environment of your essence. If you have Community around you, let them come close to you and hold you softly with their gaze or soft touches. You will know what you need. Be in the stillness of you.

To feel moved, compelled, and almost possessed. Sometimes that is exactly what we need and want. When we see a flamenco dancer, we feel their Passion. It shows a deep desire, a yearning, a compulsion to act, being inspired. It is a burning in the heart, creation, and inspiration, and compulsion to live. It is the thing that has mothers lift cars off of children, and drives men to destroy whole countries. It brings us to tears with the pain of its beauty. It is the bittersweet fleetingness of life and the deep appreciation for being moved.

We are so drawn to Passion because of our desire to feel alive. We feel it vicariously through our sports stars, as athletes eat up the field with their feet, pressing bodies against one another with what seems to be complete abandon. When you fully reclaim Passion, you reclaim a safe space to explore your wild, elegant self! You can honor all of who you are and bear witness to all the emotions you are capable of feeling without shame! You get to walk in life feeling powerful, graceful, present, and confident.

SIP
Passion Journaling Exercise

<u>If Your Passion is Wild:</u>

Where is your Passion controlling your life and burning bridges?
What part of you needs to feel heard, held, and loved?
Where do you need to break out of the limitations you've set on yourself?
What structures and support systems will help you be heard, held, and loved?

<u>If Your Passion is Dampened:</u>

Where are you stopping yourself?
Where do you need to break out of the limitations you've set on yourself?
How can you break out of these limitations?
What passions are you going to follow, and how?

Chapter Summary 19

- Sensually intelligent Passion has the rejuvenating effects of movement and expression.
- Passion is the *sempiira*, a fire built for constructive purposes.
- There is a misconception Passionate is the loss of control, and to be in control, we must suppress Passion.
- On the contrary, SQ tells us that control is deep intimacy with the body and expression, not suppression. If you are suppressing and caging something in, it means that it is out of control.
- Anger and other big emotions indicate when we have violated our values. Having a relationship with all of our emotions gives us a choice in how we will be with them, as opposed to being taken over by them.

Chapter 20

PSYCHE –
THE JOURNEY OF
THE SOUL AND SPIRIT

Element: Spirit

Characteristics: Mystical, transcendent, holy, devoted, ritual

Associated SQ Type: The Mystic

Embodied Sound: Silence. Breath. "Om"

Embodied Gesture: Hand to heart, hand to belly.

Motto: I am holy. You are holy. All is holy.

Embodiment (Body)	**Body Language**: Mind Prominent. Can feel and look not quite in the body. Either a feel of transcendence or complete groundedness and presence. Does not tend to have an in-between. **Balanced**: Sees the body as a vehicle of the divine. Treats the body as a sacred temple. Body and spirit are not separate. Emphasis on the energetic body. **Unbalanced**: Experiences the body as dangerous, profane, unnecessary. Wishes to disconnect from the body and transcend. Disconnected from the body.
Self-Love (Heart)	**Balanced**: Connected to the spirit of divine love. Universal love and compassion. God and love in all things, and self as an expression of love. Has a spiritual practice of connection. **Unbalanced**: Can be arrogant and dismissive of anyone or anything not of their belief system. "Holier than thou" attitude.
Mindfulness (Mind)	**Balanced**: "How do I bring connection to spirit and the sacred?" Able to bring perspective of the larger picture of how everything is connected. Meditates and/or prays. **Unbalanced**: "How do I protect myself from spiritual threats?" Judges, casts out, disconnects from others.
Community	**Balanced**: Spiritual way-showers. Keeps everyone connected to the spirit of the land, environment, ancestors. Creates and leads ceremonies, keeping the spirit of the community alive. Faith, compassion, goodwill toward humanity. **Unbalanced**: Disconnected from community, specifically humanity, elitist. Judgmental and dogmatic in the community.

I orgasmed for two hours from a meditating breathing exercise. The ecstatic contractions and releases happened because these were my body's best, embodied understanding of being one with everything and everything being perfect. In that experience, existence itself was perfect. Every breath, every movement, every tiny thing was perfect, and the pure wonder of that was bliss and orgasm.

I orgasmed to every breath, to time and space, to life and death, to decay and birth, to horror and beauty, and to the perfection of everything as it is. It was love-making and the creation of one-ness, the ultimate union. My body expressed the pure divinity and sacredness of it all, and ecstasy crested again and again and again and again through my being, the being of the world. All perfect and seamlessly, intricately woven into one.

How in the world did I arrive at feeling God, Source, Creation coursing through and beyond my body?

Through Psyche.

Psyche is in the realm of the intangible. It is the area of connection beyond the self, beyond the known. Psyche is concerned with the connection to spirit, god, and cosmos, devoted to the sacred connection of all. Psyche is spirit. It is the great expansiveness of space, omnipresent, omni-conscious, yet ethereal and invisible connection of all things.

When integrated with the Sensual Body Psyche provides incredibly rich, poetic, deep meaning and connection beyond our current knowledge and understanding. Faithful, devoted, spiritual, Psyche has inspired us to do incredible things for our world. These create links to our origins, history, and ancestors, to the living myths of fairies and magic, to the natural world and earth, and to space and the stars.

Priests, priestesses, and wisdom keepers are all a part of our human sensual experience. They created ritual as the embodied transmission of spirit. Through ritualized actions, we create a remembrance of the divinity of the body. The heartbeat, the in and out cadence of the breath, the bows, and murmured incantations and holy words, the candles, and altars, the gatherings that follow the cycles of the moon; all of these rituals remind the body that it is holy. Psyche is the journey of understanding and experiencing the great mystery of being alive.

Psyche out of Balance

It is easy for Psyche to get out of balance. Modern, Western society separated spirit, the divine, the sacred from the body. The practices of religion and spirituality tend to be male-dominated and patriarchal, which separate the mind and spirit from everything else. It places anything "worldly," connected to the earth, or the feminine, in a lesser echelon of importance, if not outright wrongness. The church pushed the message that the body was a place of sin and temptation. Religion justified the injustices and abuse of people of different cultures, ethnicities, races, and gender.

This separation of the body from the sacred created a rift between our bodies and our relationships with each other and our planet. It is cognitive dissonance to be taught that our bodies are made of earth, yet also our bodies are made of sin. These disconnected, "religious" doctrines have made everything to do with the body as bad, and unworthy of love and attention. Women are accused of having an evil spirit and being unclean. In many places, religion has said that bodies need to be punished, controlled, or transcended.

Overly identifying with the Psyche aspect happens a lot with people who have gone through trauma, especially sexual or connected to the body. When we exclusively depend on this aspect of self-expression, we will eject ourselves out of our body because the body does not feel like a safe place to be. One woman put it very clearly: "[I was] in an endless loop of searching for the next false ascension high. Believing that the way to enlightenment is all love and light. Not in remembrance that I am and always will be whole."

As long as we live this dissonance, we cannot live in harmony with ourselves. We as humans do inhabit bodies, and these bodies interact with the world and with others. We have emotional and physical needs: the need for attunement, reflection, and being seen.

On the other side of the spectrum of imbalance comes numbness and disconnection with the larger world. When we completely shut down and disconnect from our expression of Psyche, we experience jadedness and can get stuck in how things appear now. It can feel like being trapped in the now, uninspired, uninterested, and purposeless. The absence of interconnectedness with the larger world can feel hopeless. Yet, there is wonder to be found in the search for meaning, purpose, and connection.

The question to ask ourselves is: Is your connection to Psyche helping or hindering your relationship with yourself and your community? Is this aspect of self-expression integrated into the whole, or does it disintegrate you and cause suffering, separation, abuse, or neglect?

Reclaiming Sensual Embodied Psyche

How do we reconcile the existence of the intangible spirit in a tangible body? Where does one begin and the other end? Is it even possible to know? Is there a ghost in the machine?

When I had that spiritual, energetic orgasm, it reminded me that the body is a temple. It is our vessel for experiencing spiritual, divine union, and love. We can only understand things if we have their opposite. As cliche as it sounds, it is impossible to know light without darkness, to know love without fear, to know the interconnectedness of our souls without the separation created through having a body.

Consider your Psyche aspect like your magical self, the part of you that is a spark of the divine, an incandescent light. When you integrate and tap into this part of yourself, your social influence, allure, and the way you connect with people become magnetic. This is because you are grounded in your own body, able to connect with others on a level beyond the visible, the connection to the divine.

SIP
How to sensualize your relationship with Psyche
(Coming back to your body)

Imagine that the Psyche part of yourself is a glowing, golden web stretching from your head to the sky. Breathe deeply and feel this part of you. Put your hand to your heart, still visualizing the glowing gold from your head. With every breath, say to yourself, "This is safe. I am safe. I am home." While you speak these words, feel your body softening and opening like a flower.

I invite you to keep stretching into this, creating new neural pathways, new in your body, your heart, your spirit. Keep creating that imprint inside of you, so that it becomes more natural to you.

The more you open to, blossom, and feel the pure depths of all of your being, the more you shine. See the colors of those flowers, feel them growing roots, feel them turning up into the sunshine, to smell their scent.

Don't worry if you notice your body tightening and rejecting this. It's OK if you feel your mind rejecting the visualization of golden light. This is a part of the process. Anytime you notice tightening or discomfort in the process of self-exploration, do this:

Pause.
Breathe.
Tell yourself, "It's okay that I'm feeling _____."
"It's just a feeling. It does not define me. It is just an experience I am having."
Let yourself be.
And go back to the practice of visualization, embodied imagining.

Your experience is valid and perfect. You are on the right track because you are coming into the first steps of any change or healing journey: awareness and honoring your truth. Your body and spirit need to know that you listened, that you care, that you are paying attention before you can authentically change anything.

Your energy nourishes you and touches and inspires others. This is you opening to and integrating your brilliance so that you can be your brilliance.

Chapter 20 Summary

- Psyche is concerned with the connection to spirit, god, cosmos, and the sacred connection of everything.
- When Psyche is connected to Sensual Intelligence, it provides vibrant, poetic meaning, a sense of magic, and sacred alignment in our lives.
- When Psyche is disconnected from Sensual Intelligence, "religious" doctrines say everything to do with the body is bad.
- Without Psyche we can feel jaded, trapped in the mundanity of existence, uninspired, purposeless.
- We heal our connection through integrating our connection with spirit as an embodied experience, as our bodies are both ordinary and divinely extraordinary.

Chapter 21

PHILOSOPHY –
THE JOURNEY OF WISDOM AND TRUTH

Element: Space

Characteristics: Data and facts-driven, inquisitive

Associated SQ Type: The Intellect

Embodied Voice: "Hmmmm"

Embodied Gesture: Cross-body gestures to allow greater communication between brain hemispheres.

Motto: I learn. I know. I grow.

Embodiment (Body)	**Body Language**: Mind prominent. Somewhat unconscious body posture when in deep thought. Constant reference to the brain: neck and head stretched forward, stroking of the face on chin, brow.
	Balanced: The body as a tool to be respected and studied. Understands the inner workings of the body. Can have a precise, studied, efficient use of the body. Relaxed, yet ready.
	Unbalanced: The body is unimportant and inferior to the intellect. Ignores and neglects the body in preference for the mind.
Self-Love (Heart)	**Balanced**: Scientific and fact-driven. Balances heart and mind. Skilled at reasoning. Can connect history, patterns, and facts to support emotional health.
	Unbalanced: Mechanical, uncaring, analytical, and calculating. know-it-all, presumptive and pessimistic. Argumentative, constantly proving a point. Ignores the heart to distract from difficult emotions.
Mindfulness (Mind)	**Balanced**: "How do I find the truth? Is it measurable, empirical, and evidence-based?"
	Critical and logical thinking. Investigative. At home in the mind. Able to see patterns and habits. Problem-solution oriented.
	Unbalanced: "How do I prove that I am right? Why are they so ignorant?"
	Overanalyzing, stuck in seeing the problems, stuck in the head.
Community	**Balanced**: Truthseekers, wise counsel, provide empirical accounts of how the world and community strive. Uses data, historical references, sciences, and philosophies to create a sense of universal law, cohesion, and understanding between humanity and the environment.

	Unbalanced: Arrogance and pessimism, disconnection from community. Either recluse and become overcome with intellectual judgment and superiority that separates community and self from others.

Philosophy is concerned with understanding and explaining who we are and how things work.

The beauty of Philosophy is its ability to create a sense of coherence through research and seeing the bigger picture in a way that transcends one human body and encompasses all of life. It has a bird's-eye view and sees how everything connects as a greater whole, a greater cause than the self.

Mind Prominence

Having dependence on the mind, at the exclusion of Embodiment and Self-Love, can result in spiraling out in our thoughts. When we exclusively focus on concepts without real-world application, we distance ourselves from reality, hence the saying for academics postulating in their ivory towers. Philosophy has the perks of being a preferred method of being in our patriarchal, logic-dominated, tech-and-information world.

Philosophy can forget the heart and become so occupied with the search that it forgets to be in the world. It becomes all too easy to ignore the pure pleasure, pain, and wonder of life and be seduced into prioritizing the analytical mind, because it is valued and leads to "success". Knowledge becomes a barrier, a shield to actually feeling, to the vulnerability of not knowing. But what is the cost? What is the price of being so heavily dependent on fact, logic, and objective analysis?

The problem does not come from Philosophy but from the imbalanced dependence on the mind and the exclusion of our other types of intelligence. Dominant reliance on the mind can lead to the neglect of the body and the heart. The body is seen and experienced as superfluous, hindering progress with its needs and impulses.

However, if we completely shun Philosophy in favor of exclusively following our more emotional 7Ps, we miss out on Philosophy's ability to create universal communication. Creating an embodied relationship with Philosophy is how we reap the rewards of its wisdom. Because Philosophy focuses on ideas, it can travel into the minds of all and find the habits and patterns that connect us.

Philosophy is the web of interconnectedness, permitting us to share divergent experiences without having to experience them physically. It is not a substitute for the tangible, sensual experience. Instead, it is the connector, the communicator, that seeks to give understanding, learning, and growth to all.

How to sensualize your relationship with Philosophy

Instead of coming to quick conclusions or always seeing the world as a problem to be solved or explained, slow down and check in with yourself. When you want to explain something, or research all the facts about it, check in with your heart and ask, "What am I really searching for? Am I searching because of genuine curiosity and contribution, or is my searching a way to keep myself separated?"

The pursuit of facts can block you from the experience of the thing itself. Yes, it may feel safer to keep a distance from the messy, raw reality of the world, but always being an observer means that we really only live half a life, because you are looking through a window, rather than coming fully into the room.

Sensualizing Philosophy means turning that investigative lens on your own heart, vulnerability, and the things you do not and cannot know, and simply sitting in the mystery of it.

Ask yourself vulnerable, heart-focused questions. What do you yearn to know the answer to, *especially* if it is in the area of your body, intimacy, or the heart? Ask yourself the question, write it down, even. And then, sit with it.

Don't answer the questions. Instead, sit with the inquiry without trying to make sense of it, solve it, find a solution.

Ask the question and feel what part of your body activates? Is it your chest? Your stomach? Your throat?

How does it activate? Does it tighten, tremble, stiffen?

Just be with this sensation. Do not try to fix it or turn this into a research project.

Sit and be with it.

Breathe. Notice your breathing. Notice your entire body as it engages with the question, with the very act of not knowing and not trying to know.

As we sit with the not knowing, without doing anything, we open to compassion. Compassion literally means to feel the pain with something. In this case, compassion is toward yourself, opening your heart to being in the unknown.

It's time to trust that you have created this wall of data and facts, you are safe. Now it's time to put all those "facts" to the test, and just let go.

Take advice from Passion (Chapter 19), take refuge in Peace (Chapter 23), and explore the world with Pleasure (Chapter 17).

Chapter 21 Summary
- Philosophy is our understanding and explaining who we are and how things work.
- It has the ability to create coherence through research and data.
- Dominant reliance on the characteristics of Philosophy leads to neglect of the body and the heart.
- Sensualizing Philosophy means turning that investigative and inquisitive lens on your own body and heart and being open to the mystery of not knowing.

Chapter 22

POWER –
THE JOURNEY OF
BOUNDARIES AND STRUCTURE

Just because you sit on a throne and you have a crown, does not make you a king, queen, or ruler. It makes you a person sitting on a big chair wearing a heavy hat.

Element: Metal

Characteristics: Self-reliant, Structured, Magnetic

Associated SQ Type: The Domme

Embodied Voice: Ohh!

Embodied Gesture: Feet wide, knees bent to 90 degrees, curve your arms open wide as if in a big bear hug.

Motto: Stand your ground, baby, cause no one else is going to do it for you.

Embodiment (Body)	**Body Language:** Body takes up space, even without physically taking up space. Controlled, deliberate, and purposeful. There are no extra or unnecessary gestures.
	Balanced: The body creates safety, structure, container, order. Solid Presence. Calm, seen, and heard. Strength.
	Unbalanced: Overbearing, domineering, clenching, grinding, and tension, Immovable, protected, and closed off. Difficulty allowing self to be held physically.
Self-Love (Heart)	**Balanced:** Can galvanize structure and coherence even in emotionally charged situations. Calm in the middle of a storm. Create emotional safety through clear boundaries.
	Unbalanced: Controlling, strict, tyrannical, lack of empathy and compassion, cut off emotionally. Uses nit-picking, perfectionism, workaholism, and controlling measures to distract from difficult emotions. Difficulty feeling emotional vulnerability, recognizing the need for support and love, especially for themselves.
Mindfulness (Mind)	**Balanced:** "How do I bring order and efficiency?"
	Clear-headed. logical and rational, step by step. clear and commanding communication.
	Unbalanced: "How do I get in control?"
	Manipulative, scheming, calculating. "I will not be controlled," "It's lonely at the top," lone wolf feeling.

Community	**Balanced**: The steadfast and purposeful leader. Helps others find their way with clarity and directness. People look up to this person. Instills a sense of trust and stewardship of community and environment. Sees how to bring humanity and nature together in a constructive way.
	Unbalanced: Exploits nature and people. Seeks to control, use, and extract energy resources from people and the environment. Sees community as something to rule and bend to their will.

My friend and colleague, Mistress Z, invited me to lead the embodiment portion of her workshop. It was a Dominatrix training weekend. She is a pro-Domme (a professional Dominatrix) and was teaching women how to channel their inner Dominatrix.

The women came for different reasons. Some wanted to enter the profession; others wanted to spice up their love life, while others just wanted to experience their power. Where else would be more fun, fitting, and sexy than with a Dominatrix!?

Mistress Z had taken these women to her dungeon. They dressed in reds and blacks, leather and corsets, and played with her many paddles, whips, restraints, and other toys. They were gathered in a brightly lit sunshine room, with white sheepskin rugs and comfortable couches when I met them, a far cry from the dungeon. The women were a mixture of titillated, excited, scared, and nervous. Some looked like they were putting on a brave show but were totally out of their league.

Mistress Z knew my work, and she understood that it was one thing to mentally know the philosophy and have the tools of the Domme. It is another thing to authentically have the embodiment and presence of a Domme.

That's where I came in.

My job was to take them from a mental understanding and performing of a Dominatrix to owning and embodying their Domme. I'm not Domme, but as an embodiment expert, I know that the mind cannot believe what the body does not feel. These women could listen, read, and study about what a Domme was. They could gain an in-depth, mental understanding of the history of Power dynamics. They could dress the part, use the tools and toys, and go through the motions, but none of this could ever give them what they truly desired: to reclaim the Power that societal norms had taken from them.

Sensually Intelligent Power is the expression of boundaries and structure within ourselves and our interactions with others. It is a journey of sovereignty and how we create and occupy space.

I love teaching workshops on embodied power dynamics. The kink community is not the only place to explore power dynamics, but it is one of the most enjoyable ways to delve in because you get to play!

I'll briefly share how I led this group into an authentic embodiment of Power and their inner Dominatrix. I encourage you to do more than just read this section. Follow along! Do it with us. Take this opportunity to explore your relationship with Power.

Step 1) The first thing I did was ask: "What does Power look like for you? What is your *real* relationship with Power?"

This is always an essential first step in any embodiment activity. While we think that we can just learn new information and put it on like an article of clothing, it's not that simple. We first have to lean in and get intimate with our inner truth and conditioning. Our preconceived notions come from societal expectations. As a result, these expectations become lodged into our bodies.

If we try to learn something new from our conditioned body state, we will literally be fighting against everything we learned to keep us safe and accepted. (And there's nothing less acceptable than a woman owning and embodying her Power.) So get honest with yourself. Own your truth right now.

How does your body, heart, and mind experience Power?

Step 2) After unpacking the real stories of our relationship with Power, I lead them through an embodied release practice. This allows us to shake off, to disembody the shackles of our conditioning.

"Pay attention to the words you used to speak about yourself and Power. Now put your attention on your body. How does your body feel when you share your Power story? Pay attention to any tightness or tension. What changed in your body?

"Now, without words, ask your body what it needs to release this story. What does your body need to let go of this belief that has been shaping your life?

Now move! Let it move through and out of your body. Don't forget to use your voice, too!"

What we believe shapes our bodies and how we use our bodies. If one person's belief around Power is "I'm not allowed to have it, but I still want it," and another person's belief is "I'm afraid of power because my romantic partner left me when I stood up for myself, and now I am alone," these two people will have a different embodied relationship with Power. Our different embodied beliefs shape how we speak, move, act, and perceive. So we use the body to shake, thrust, undulate, punch, stomp, scream, and sob to move that story out of the body. (This is true for *any* of the sensual expressions!)

Step 3) After releasing, I told them, "Stop. Be still. Breathe. Just feel yourself. Feel the space in your body. Feel the buzzing inside of you. This feeling, this space, is the shape of *you*. Now you get to feel, imagine and embody what Power means for you.

"How does Power manifest in your body? How does it make you breathe? How does it make you walk? How does it make you sit, talk, smell, take up space, lick your lips, and be in the world? How do you beautifully embody this place of fullness?"

But what *is* this place of fullness? What are the characteristics of Power through the lens of Sensual Intelligence, and how does it shape our bodies, lives, and relationships?

Characteristics of Power

Sensually Intelligent Power is not just the ability to simply act; it is the ability to work in harmony, growth, sustainability, integrity, integration, and love. In addition, sensually Intelligent Power is discerning and healing.

People mistakenly regard Power as a one-directional, outward force; however, Power requires that we embody both dominance and submission—the push and the give. It has sensitivity, nuance, the ability to self-reflect and reflect to others because it sees itself, and sees itself in others. In other words, Power is both felt *and* given. It is a gift that keeps giving, not a pestilence that strips people.

Sensually Intelligent Power is artistry, a composition that includes all the parts and has them work together in their unique way. Power self-corrects and forgives because it is steeped in inner knowledge.

The element of Power is metal. Metal has structure, but can also accept new forms. When metal is hit with pressure and heat, it will initially resist. However, with sustained pressure and heat, metal becomes molten and can be shaped. When it hardens, it is even more powerful than its raw unforged form.

Sensually intelligent Power understands what it means to yield and submit as well as when to resist. If it does not, it will shatter. When we are put under heat and pressure (stress, challenges, hardships), a healthy relationship with Power allows us to withstand the pressure or transform ourselves if needed. We become something new and stronger.

One of the best embodiments of sensually intelligent power is the pregnant woman. The womb is both incredibly powerful and pliable. Pregnancy is deeply sensual, the senses are heightened, the body is forced to connect with nature. The womb is self-reliant, strong, yet malleable. Power is magnetic and able to withstand outside forces and hold a stable, sound structure because it is connected to the magnetic field in the heart.

Power-less?

People tend to fall on either side of the spectrum of Power. They avoid Power because of how they see it corrupting others. Or they feel burdened by too much Power and responsibility.

Lack of Power means lack of boundaries and structures. This is unsafe. When you do not have a clear "yes" and "no" it makes it impossible for others to create trust in your world. You can do things you don't want to do, be easily influenced by others, and feel that others are asking too much of you. You may avoid confrontation because it feels uncomfortable, scary, out of control, or too big. If you live life trying not to rock the boat, upset anyone, or not put yourself out there, then where are you? You don't ever get to exercise your assertiveness.

Pay attention if you have a habit of staying in a relationship that you need to leave, romantic or professional. When you don't claim your Power, you don't claim your voice. There is no declaration of your needs, rather a go-with-the-flow kind of vibe, which is great—except for when you never get your needs met.

People cut themselves off when they enter the realm of claiming authority because it brings up uncomfortable and unfamiliar sensations. It's vulnerable to admit you want to be in control when you never have. That way of being simply is not in the body.

I get a lot of women-identified or feminine people saying, "I'm afraid that if I show too much Power then no one is going to love or care for me." They practiced being safe by being small, so putting themselves out there by standing up for themselves feels like a threat to their existence. It is difficult to look at how much power they give away in a relationship and how they change to adapt to that relationship.

If you are in this situation, ask yourself, are you sacrificing your wants, needs, and genuine expression to have love and connection? If so, what are you and others missing out on by *you* not being there?

Sensually Intelligent Power gives the ability to create boundaries, adapt and change as circumstances need, and create the most optimal way of being and relating with oneself and others. For example, the kink community has a term for this dynamic, D/s (Dominant/submissive). In a healthy D/s relationship, there are boundaries that the submissive partner puts in place that the Dominant partner, despite being the one who appears to have the power, will never cross. These boundaries allow for a much better relationship than relationships without boundaries. Another wonderful example is in romantic relationships. A couple can set a boundary by agreeing Thursday is date night. This means that planning anything else on date night is crossing the boundary.

SIP
Balancing Power within you

Journal and Reflection

When was the last time you let your power go?
When you did not stand for what you knew was your truth?
Where did you feel it in your body?
How did it feel?
What actions did you take as a result?

When did you stand for what you knew was your truth?
Where did you feel it in your body?
How did it feel?
What actions did you take as a result?

Breathe in.
Breathe out.

Just be with this knowledge. Repeat this exercise to gain familiarity with your relationship to Power.

Toxic Power

Power without Sensual Intelligence is rigid, forbidding, and demanding. Someone very heavy on their Power can feel cold and dismissive. Others may see you as too structured and controlled. You do not feel approachable because there are too many rules to engage with you. It can feel hard to get truly intimate with you because you do not let them in. You can feel exacting, controlling, and guarded.

The culture of leadership today is hierarchical and linear. It encourages self-negligence, distance from emotions, and isolation. Phrases like "It's lonely at the top" and "absolute power corrupts absolutely" linguistically express the shape, feel, and purpose of power. When leadership is not informed by Sensual Intelligence can become exploitative, oppressive, and unjust.

I watched a documentary about Harvey Weinstein that made my stomach sick and brought me back to that office in Arkansas, with my abusive mentor, at 16 years old. Harvey Weinstein was a prominent American film producer and then convicted sex offender. He was found to have sexually abused scores of women and girls over the years, exploiting his power and people's desire to become successful in the world of film.

In the clip, a young woman was doing a pitch for Harvey Weinstein. I felt my eyes go blurry. I could have been her, and she could have been me. Every word she spoke and gesture she made, he manipulated and intrusively sexualized. She was palpably uncomfortable in her attempts to keep the situation safe and under control. He was striking and retreating like a clever snake. She was like a cornered mouse, frozen with fear and confusion, yet still trying to do a good job and pretend his sexual advances were not happening. Everything about the interaction shows what happens when our society operates without Sensual Intelligence and abuses Power.

Our system says we need to suffer before we get freedom or payment. The price of admission to play in the game is our Power and sovereignty.

Conditioning has created a perfect Petri dish for the victim-perpetrator dynamic. If boys are taught not to feel their feelings, they grow up not feeling their feelings and are less likely to have empathy, compassion, and sensual connection to themselves and others. Is it any wonder that he ignores her feelings when he's been told his entire life to ignore his own?

If girls are taught to be nice, accommodating, and quiet, they grow up taking care of everyone else at the expense of their voice. As a result, they are less likely to be assertive, sovereign, and *own* their sensuality and bodies. Is it any wonder that she ignores her boundaries and truth when she's been told this her entire life?

The victim-perpetrator dynamic I shared above is an extreme but not farfetched. I don't say this to blame or excuse anyone's behavior but rather to illuminate the mechanisms that support the power dynamics under which we operate. Whether or not this dynamic plays out to the full extent in which I shared, the truth is that this pattern of behavior underscores our every interaction, with varying ranges of subtlety. Every time a woman's voice is ignored, and she's told that she's being too emotional, this dynamic is in play. Every time a man is told to suck it up and stop acting like a pussy, this dynamic is in play.

Harvey Weinstein is just one of many people in "power" who have perpetuated this same offense again and again. This is a product of a society that values profit over humanity and has no Sensual IQ.

Power is the intelligence of boundaries and structure. Watching Harvey Weinstein and this young woman in the macabre dance, it became clear that this interaction resulted from missing SQ. If we give our women and girls, our men and boys, access to their sensuality, they can have a relationship with their whole integrated selves. Then, I believe this type of shit would not be so pervasive.

I wish I had been taught how to love, protect, and celebrate my body and my whole self. Instead, I was taught to obey the rules and ignore the wisdom of my soma. But that is why I am here. I've learned through experience and healed through an intense examination of how Sensual Intelligence can help us regain balance and joy in our relationships.

This shift is not going to happen overnight. We must reimagine cultural practices through the lens of Sensual Intelligence so we can rebuild an equitable world.

Reclaiming and Healing Power

> ### Body Prayer
>
> My body is sovereign.
> My body is wise.
> When I listen to my body's wisdom, I heal.
> I reveal my true voice
> And claim myself as my own.
>
> Body Movements for each line of the poem:
>
> *(Wide leg stance, arms open wide)*
> *(Brings hands together in prayer)*
> *(Cross movements like you're gathering.*
> *Long Caress down the body)*
> *(Hands on hips and swirl both directions.)*
> *(Big circle gathering up all energy; bring it to the heart)*
>
> This specific set of movements will allow you to embody sovereignty.

Quite a few women in leadership will laud the merits of feminine leadership yet want to distance themselves from their bodies because they want to be seen as respectable and credible. We still have much to develop in our journey of fully reclaiming holistic, embodied leadership. When we are unbalanced in our power, something feels off, and we will go in our heads to try to make it right, make sense of it, talk it away, or justify it.

However, if you want to feel the power of your own body, you have to own your story. Create a practice of connecting with your body, because your body already has its own connection to its story.

If you are the one who has been on the side of feeling powerless, you have permission to write your own story and include yourself as the main character. When you allow others to write your story, you do not give yourself a voice for who you are and what you stand for.

If you are on the other side of Power and are overwhelmed by the sheer amount of responsibility you have and everyone depending on you, no more of this. No more thinking that in order to receive the love you have to give so much that you don't even know yourself.

If you feel like you had no choice and responsibility was forced upon you, if you are keeping everything and everyone together, it's time to soften the grip and let go of the tight reins of control you put on every aspect of your life to keep you safe.

You get to realize you are soft and sensitive. Learn from Pleasure, Play, and Peace. They will teach you that there's no shame in being soft and sensitive.

Your Power is not compromised by your feeling into your vulnerability. It is enhanced because you can be more sensitive. Surrender and savor this moment. You don't always have to be strong and impenetrable. I know some of you have never been able to experience that for yourself before.

You have full permission to take this moment to breathe, feel, and celebrate yourself exactly as you are.

I took Mistress Z's women on an embodiment journey, helping them tap into their unique expression of Power and dominance that nourished them and was real, not performed.

We ended by bowing down on our knees, faces to the ground, supplicated, our hands pointing toward one woman at a time, her time.

One by one, each woman took her turn to stand above us, fully embodied, in ravishing, deliciously poised, self-love. Each woman had her chance to stand in lush, grounded, powerful, sensual womanhood. Feeling herself, dancing, loving herself. Seeing herself as the sensually embodied and powerful being that she is. Holding within her the masculine *and* the feminine, the Dominant and submissive, the light and the dark, the soft and jagged, and everything in between.

We bowed down to each woman, reverently whispering her name again and again.

Their Power had awoken.

Chapter 22 Summary

- Power is directive and purposeful. It has structure but can also accept a new form when under lots of pressure and heat—like metal.
- Power without sensual intelligence is blocky, rigid, and demanding.
- Lack of Powers leads to poor self-boundaries and structure. You can do things that you don't really want to do.
- To feel the Power of your own body, you have to own your story. You do this by owning your past story and then imagining and embodying something new.

Chapter 23

PEACE –
THE JOURNEY OF INNER TRANQUILITY AND NOURISHMENT

Peace

Peace was ethereal. Everywhere and nowhere all at once as it touched my body and melted like cotton candy in my mouth. Like a petal, like dandelion fluff in the wind, landing in the black cotton of my hair. It caressed my softness and whispered in the silence.

I breathed in deeply and allowed Peace to open me, caressing my insides with a soft murmur.

Element: Water

Characteristics: Fluid, nourishing, harmonizing, healing

Associated SQ Type: The Empath

Embodied Voice: Ahhhh

Embodied Gesture: Gentle, loving caress with the front and back of fingertips along the cheek. Self-hug with soft rocking

Motto: Hold me, love me, keep me safe, touch me softly

Embodiment (Body)	**Body Language:** Self-Love/Heart prominent. The body is fluid and flowing, gentle touch. Soft sighs, speech is comforting. **Balanced:** Nurturing; soft, melodic voice; healing and restorative hands and body. Uses mirroring to make others feel at ease and listened to. Adept with mirror neurons. **Unbalanced:** The body internally and externally collapsed, slumped, and weak. Can cry a lot.
Self-Love (Heart)	**Balanced:** Spacious, fluid, flowing, gentle and soft touch, nurturing. Unafraid to look at the shadow aspects and be with grief, sorrow, and other emotions of heartache. Allows vulnerability, softness, unhurried healing. "All in good time." **Unbalanced:** Smothering, weak, no structure or boundaries, allowing (too much); passive. Feelings easily hurt. Very sensitive to criticism. Can indulge in and become a victim to difficult emotions. Martyrdom.
Mindfulness (Mind)	**Balanced:** "How do I bring ease, harmony, and flow?" Diplomat of the heart. Brings empathy, compassion, love, and forgiveness.

	Unbalanced: "How do I protect myself against everyone? How do I stay safe?" Passive-aggressive. Avoids conflict. Would rather be the victim or the martyr than assert needs.
Community	**Balanced**: Healers and midwives/guides of transformation. Sensitive to human relationships and the environment. Peacekeepers, bridge makers, teaching and embodying compassion, empathy, forgiveness. **Unbalanced**: "Good girl/good boy." Source of sorrow and misery, self-absorbed, sadness, and depression. Can become isolated because of overwhelm and hopelessness, or be exhausted from overgiving and over-identifying with others.

Peace is the great surrender—the perfect embrace. It is being at home within your heart, the still-moving waters in which we submerge ourselves to remember who we are. Through Peace, we join with ourselves and nourish the heart's desire.

Peace is the gift of beauty we give to ourselves. Even just one moment of pure self-acceptance, one moment of no self-judgment will create a balm of healing. When we realize that there is no need to fix, change, prove, or improve ourselves, something inside of us shifts. We go from the rigidity of effort to the gentle waters of love.

Peace is not the opposite of movement and striving. Rather, it is what will get you in touch with the dance of your internal world. The internal stillness teaches us to love, care for, and accept with the same fluidity as the river washing over the rocks.

Peace says, "Simply be, and accept who you are."

Peace Out of Balance

Our deepest desire and greatest need in life are to belong and to be accepted. We spend a lifetime changing and molding ourselves to fit in and be accepted. Our primal brain learned that if we are not accepted, we will be cut off from the tribe without resources or protection and die from social or physical starvation. We feel this as children and go to great lengths to earn the love and acceptance of our guardians, even if those guardians are too damaged to love us correctly.

People pleasers, saviors, and martyrs are manifestations of when Peace gets out of balance. Mothers and caregivers are especially vulnerable to falling into this category simply by living in this country. As we all follow the beat of the independence drum and silently march to the tune of "Pull yourself up by the bootstraps because you're on your own," unbalanced Peace will lead us to try to save and take care of everyone alone, with no respite. However, when we do this, we develop anxiety, feelings of not being deserving, and that we have to work for everything to go right all of the time.

Ironically, the things the Peace provides for others, Peace will forget to provide for itself when out of balance. This part of us forgets that we also have needs, and we, too, need to feel a depth of safety and security in our hearts and bodies.

That heavy pressure of obligation, holding it all together, keeping everyone calm and on good terms, is like damming up a river. When we dam up ourselves and our self-expression, our flow of Peace for ourselves and others, it feels like a heavy compression around the heart.

Still waters stagnate. Waters that flow without being replenished by the rain will dry up and cease to exist. The invitation to those who are out of balance with Peace is to reconnect to the sensual reality of living waters.

> **SIP**
> **Peace Journaling**
>
> There are parts of our bodies, hearts, and ways of being that we are not OK with; parts of ourselves where we have been secretly saying, "You do not deserve to be here. You should not be here." When we learn to love and accept them exactly as they are, it is those parts that will allow us to soften.
>
> What is/are the part(s) of you that needs you to say, "I see you, I love you, I accept you as you are"?

Healing Peace

> Waves of Peace
>
> *Riding the waves was so soothing and felt like beauty inside my body.*
> *It made me catch my breath and sway with delight.*
> *I let the ocean be the lead and I just let my hips follow.*
> *Me and the ship and the whales below,*
> *All in the ecstatic throes of nature's beauty and pleasure.*

The energy of Peace is nourishing, like that of a mother, a guardian. They provide safety and support so that the child can explore, discover, be curious, learn, and safely experience life. It is in our nature to want to explore and discover our world, to experiment. And without the intelligence of Peace, we cannot allow ourselves that deep inquiry, the softness, a place in which to land, accept, and be.

When Peace forgets her beauty and divinity, she becomes downtrodden and resentful. Sensually embodied Peace is the queen of the waters, like the Yoruba goddess of the ocean, Yemanja, relentless in her abundance. She remembers to tend to and drink from the sweet nectar that gushes between her thighs. She is the sweet waters of amrita herself.

In French, the term for orgasm is *la petite mort*, which literally translates to "small death." This is the most accurate phrase for the explosion of ecstasy and pleasure inside our bodies. Orgasm and climax cannot happen until there is la petite mort, biologically, a shutting down of the brain. Great and utter peace. A stillness, safety, and nourishment in which the entire being surrenders because it feels safe.

Especially for women, this stillness, silence, and deep surrender give space for a rush of fire and sensation, the exclamations of ecstasy, and the wild rush of bliss.

When I lead any workshop, I will *always* end with Peace, because especially as we try to survive our culture, the child part of us gets sacrificed. I assume that every person has a little child part of them that really needs to hear and feel: Hold me, love me, keep me safe, touch me softly.

We have been so conditioned to be hard, protect ourselves, guard our bodies and our hearts that we neglect to connect with ourselves or each other.

Peace is about giving space and permission for life to enter in all its complex shapes and structures. It is to feel your growth by truly providing freedom to be yourself, exactly as you are, be it sad, furious, lost, insecure, confused, or stubborn. You can quit being a martyr to your circumstances, to your obligations. You have choice and can choose to nourish yourself. You can never be forced as long as you embody the fullness of Peace.

Peace is the love and self-acceptance of the mother archetype. The nourishing softness and unconditional acceptance allow you to rest your head and body. Peace is mighty. It will get you in touch with your inner world and innate beauty like nothing else will.

Try speaking this intention to yourself: "I commit to be present with myself and share my heart with love. I allow myself to relax and let go. I honor my traumas and hardships, but I do not cling to the stories of how they define me. I take the time to be still with the inner wisdom of my heart. I know peace when I am with myself. My heart opens up and surrenders."

> ### SIP: Peace
> ### Going on a journey of peace
> ### 5–20 minute journey
>
> Use this practice to bring Peace to your body and your nervous system.
>
> Dim the lights and sit or lay comfortably.
>
> Allow yourself to soften; breathe deeply.
>
> Feel your breath come in and out of your body. The pace doesn't matter; just breathe.
>
> Pay attention to the coolness of the air as it passes through your nostrils and mixes with the warm essence of your throat, lungs, and belly. Be with the breath that is warmed inside of you.
>
> Listen to the lullaby of your breathing and start to hum. Whatever melody comes from your body, as long as it is inspired by the rise and fall of your chest, and the beating of your heart, is the right melody.
>
> It can be completely tuneless, because even something tuneless to the conscious brain, may actually be the melody of your heart, of your Peace. The point is that the hum should come from your connection to your body, the rhythm and dance of the air as it enters your lungs and dances with your internal organs.
>
> When you exhale that breath, your life's air, part of you lingers and floats in the atmosphere, sharing its memories, experiences, and gifts. Know that every exhale is the gift of you. The gift of your breath, your voice, your essence shared out into the world.
>
> Now, take a moment and ask yourself: Where do I need love, nourishment? Feel into the core of your body. Now imagine your breath, your life's blood, your nourishing waters touching that part of you.

If you can, put your hands on that part of your body, feeling the flow of your own liquids. Then ask that part of you, "What do you need? How do you want to be nourished?"

Listen. Truly listen with your heart. Listen to your own body as you would listen to a loved one.

Respond "Thank you," and then do as your body requested.

Repeat this until your heart, your body, your whole being is flowing with Peace.

Chapter 24

INTIMACY, EROS, AND RELATIONSHIPS

> Want
>
> *What if, my love, I took my pain, doubt, and fear and fed it to the ocean?*
> *What if I let the water cool my rage, and soak this raw heart in a basin of deep healing ritual?*
> *What if I allowed this dark hot fire to purge the fear from my soul, and I howled from the sad mad woman wrestling deep within myself?*
> *What if I basked in the heat of my own deep yearning, sweating out the sweet scent of my desire, and the pure love of my heart?*
>
> *What if I did not need you anymore, my love?*
> *What if I only wanted you?*
>
> (Watch this poem as a dance video: https://youtu.be/cPDiPbWrT40)

I've participated in my fair share of workshops to enhance sexuality, power, and creating loving relationships. The sexual workshops tend to emphasize the genitalia as the one source of creativity and expression. There is a place for this form of empowerment, but it is limited in its scope and expression. On the other hand, many relationship workshops gloss over embodiment, saying that if communication and companionship are there, then the sexual connection will also occur.

If you go to any class about sex, sexuality, or relationships between the masculine and the feminine, you will often see this time and time again: a cluelessness from the masculine about sensitivity, softness, and slowing down; and a reluctance, fear, from the feminine of stepping into and claiming their power. Obviously, this is oversimplified but too common to not mention. The roles that we take on, and the power dynamics that we fall into without question, result from a lifetime of training and practicing how to be disconnected and disembodied from our truth.

Sensuality sets the frame. Sensuality is an honoring of our bodies and the act of creation we engage through our bodies. It requires us to slow down, to be present, to feel each nuance of touch, taste every molecule of sweat, to hear and revel in the changing sound of their breath and the symphony of skin, sweat, and friction, because these are connected to the heart and the mind.

Sensuality requires us to honor and revel in the artistry of our bodies.

So often, people will *perform* sexuality. The feminine will perform pleasure. The masculine will perform prowess. They do what they think is expected of them: be a good girl, be a virile man, and make things go smoothly and appear correct. "We went through all the right moves, right?" They perform their "pleasure" so often that they have no idea whether there ever was pleasure, for them, at all. They don't know that there was a way to truly revel in one's own body, one's skin, to feel the deep erotic power of themselves.

If you have ever "performed" sex because you were not into it, or doing it out of obligation or responsibility, or checked out so you could just get through it, you were disembodied. The sad truth is that some people have experienced such trauma in their own bodies, that being in their body feels like the ultimate danger.

Intimacy is closeness, and the only way to get close is to let down protective walls that separate us. Eros opens us to the portal of the divine, reminding us that all life can be an erotic wake-up call if we choose it to be. A relationship is an art of practicing connecting in the ever-changing dance of communication.

All of these belong in Sensual Intelligence, and Sensual Intelligence belongs in intimacy, eros, and relationships. It is the life glue that makes our internal work and external world make sense. Sensual Intelligence allows us to live, grow, and transform so we can be co-creators of life.

People want to feel powerful, yet still soft and worthy of being loved and cared for. We want to feel joy and freedom, to play and be silly, but the fear of not being taken seriously holds us back. We want to feel pleasure beyond our wildest dreams and be totally uninhibited, but we can't accept ourselves as someone who is that wild. It's scary, it's "unacceptable," it's vulnerable, and we want it, but we don't want it. The practice of Sensual Intelligence is about authenticity, presence, and integration as the foundations for love, joy, and eros. New, empowered relating has to be continuously and sensually taught.

Sensual IQ and Relationships

It does not matter what kind of relationship it is: romantic, friendly, professional, or familial, for relationships to work *for us*, we must show up fully present and aware. So, if you have not already, I invite you to take the SQ Quiz (http://www.Shawnrey.com/Quiz). And, *especially* for relationships, ask the person you are in a relationship with to take it for you and vice versa.

Healthy relationships are reciprocal: as you nourish and heal yourself, you nourish and heal your partnership, and in turn, your partnership nourishes and heals you. The problem happens when either party blames the other and stops the process. If you are waiting for a partner to show up and love you 'correctly,' but you are not working on loving and expressing yourself, you will not be prepared to take full advantage of a delicious, juicy partnership, even if the perfect person showed up at your doorstep. The level of connectedness and presence we have with ourselves is the level of connectedness and presence we can bring to a relationship.

When we know ourselves, we can invite others to dance with us. Dance with yourself. Learn your own body. Dance your life and relationships.

When you dance in a relationship with a partner, there is trust in their capability to be with themselves and to be with you, and your ability to be with yourself.

We will stumble, even fall, but if we're both committed to the dance of relationship, we both bring our training and awareness of self and others, plus our unique style, rhythm, and expression.

Look at yourself and ask: Am I ready? Have I learned to dance with myself, to listen to my body and my needs? Or am I depending on others to bring the magic and hold me up?

Dance is listening. Listen to your body, heart, and truth. Listen to another's truth.

Listen to your resistance when the truth is not what you want to hear.

Dance is communication and connection, where we connect with love, expansion, admiration, and trust.

SIP
Dance Your Relationship using SQ

Knowing your Sensual IQ can help you and your partner know where you each are. This way, you can start having conversations and exploring activities that can support where you are in your sensual journey.

As always, the first step is to have awareness. Where are you and your partner expressed or suppressed in your Sensual Body? Is one of you more embodied, heart-centered, or mind-centered? Is your partner a Diva, and is low on the Self-Love areas? Are you a Domme?

Take the assessment and discuss the results using these questions.

Bonus: Let your partner-friend take the test for you. See how they experience you.

- How do we get back up and learn from the mistakes, but not let the mistakes and pain from the past block our love, joy, and openness?
- How can we open our hearts, trust, and be smart?

We can look and understand how things fall apart, communicate on how to keep the communication and connection, and start to learn how we dance together.

Sensually Intelligent Sensual Massage

You can use the 7Ps of Sensual Expression in all parts of your relationship. When we apply Sensual Intelligence in our relationships, we reclaim a sense of wonder. Vitality, kinesthetic exploration, self-discovery, and self-mastery, unlock sensual awareness.

One fun way that I do it in mine is through sensual massage—a sensually intelligent massage. Everything in our journey has laid the foundation for you to explore different types of touch and arouse and activate pleasure and connection. Getting in touch with your senses, with your body, gives you greater access to your mind, emotions, connection, and pleasure.

When I facilitate sensual touch and massage workshops or guide sensual embodied awakening circles, we do not solely focus on pleasure and feeling good. Sensual Intelligence permeates all of life, and a sensually intelligent massage is just a concentrated laboratory to

- explore curiosity and openness (Play)
- create structure and boundaries (Power)
- discovering how we move with the emotions of our bodies (Passion)
- create a safe space for nourishment, compassion, and flow (Peace)

- connect to the power of sacred, ritual, ceremony (Psyche)
- be deliberate and observant in our technique and partner's response (Philosophy).

Here is how to use the 7Ps to do a Sensually Intelligent massage. This can be a self-massage or with another person.

Power

Prepare the space, both your physical space and your mental space. Make sure the area is clean, safe, and inviting. Set aside, at the very least, 30 minutes. Give yourself time in the end for integration.

Don't cheat and turn the massage into a sexual encounter. Just don't do it. This violates consent. Trust, communication, and staying with your word is all in the realm of Power.

Psyche

Set an intention for why you are doing this massage. Is it to create more closeness and connection? See this time that you have set aside for the massage as sacred. See the body you are going to touch as holy. Bless the room, the hands that will touch, and the body that will be touched. Send a prayer of gratitude for the ability to share such a beautiful and intimate act.

Pleasure

Is the music beautiful? Do the colors and the oils bring delight to your senses? When you touch, take your time. Savor the miracle of life underneath your hands. Allow your entire body to feel the delight of this moment and the next moment. Slow down. You can always go even slower.

Passion

What emotions do you notice coming up when you are touching or being touched? Invite them in. Be open to growling, moaning, and riding the waves of the fire. Be the *sempiira*. Is there a desire for scratching, or slapping, or grabbing the flesh and giving it more vigorous attention? But make sure you are still connected to your heart, breath, and consent. Remember, consent is sensual. Breathe.

Play

Be open-minded and bring your curiosity. You don't have to be so serious. Explore the body and have fun!

Philosophy

Pay attention to their body, using a soft mind. Don't overthink it. Just allow your researcher, your observer, to take notes through your embodied touch. The body is intelligent. Just let it speak, body to body.

Peace

Pause. Be still. Breathe. Take a moment and just let yourself be held and taken care of. When you touch, you are both the giver and the receiver. When you are touched, you are both the receiver and the giver. Allow your body to be the ocean. If tears form, let them fall. Softly stroke their cheek and lovingly cradle their face. Relax, receive, and let your breath be the waves of the sea. When you embrace, just let yourself be in complete surrender and acceptance. You do not have anywhere you need to be, and nothing you need to do except be here right now. You deserve it.

Later, check with your Sensual Body by following these steps.

Embodiment

What is your body feeling? Where do you feel softness or tension? What has shifted? Breathe.

Self-Love

How is your heart? What emotions came up for you? Where did you feel them? Every emotion you feel is valid. Just allow it to be.

Mindfulness

What thoughts did you notice or are you noticing right now as you reflect on your experience? Remember, mindfulness is the mind's natural abilities plus embodied awareness. Breathe and feel into your body first before answering.

The sensually intelligent massage is a way to find joy, passion, pleasure, excitement, peace in our bodies, and the ability to have amazing body, heart, and mind orgasms. It gives you the power to create embodied, erotic, and heart-centered intimacy.

Chapter 24 Summary

- If we do pleasure, orgasm, and relationship work before learning the foundation of our senses and joyful embodiment, our joy will not last. It will be like putting icing on a shit cake.
- People often *perform* sex, intimacy, and sensuality instead of opening to the vulnerability it requires.
- Sensuality is an honoring of our bodies. It requires us to slow down, be present, and be honest.
- We can use the 7Ps of Sensual Expression in all parts of relationships.
- When we apply Sensual Intelligence in our relationships, we reclaim a sense of wonder and trust.

CONCLUSION

Home Within

I move with the liquid rhythm of my blood
And the unrushed drum of my heart
I dance to whale song and the symphony of ocean waves
I moan sounds of exaltation
Mouth widening, a cavern expanding,
A yawn of "Ahhhhh"
Stretching the corners of my lips
The slick edges of my womb
And pulling a smile to my cheeks

I allowed myself to birth myself
Into the home of my own body, the home of my own skin
To love the feel of my body as I draw in
My first
Sweet tastes
Of life air

I welcome myself
Open to my body
Open to my heart
Inside and out
I am open and primed for pleasure and sensation
Awaken
Awakening
Awake

I am home
I am whole
I am wholly home
I am holy home.

Five years ago, Gina and I met at a gathering and I shared about my Sensual Intelligence work. She contacted me soon afterward and shared with me that she wanted to "get better at sex." Her husband was telling her that she was a lazy lover and not passionate in bed. Not only was she dealing with an absent, unsupportive husband, but she also had a child who was having trouble in school. The cherry on top was that she was totally unsatisfied with her accounting job and was just feeling lost. She figured that she could make herself more passionate and rekindle her relationship with her husband.

The first thing I invited Gina to do was to create an embodied self-loving ritual, like the solo version of the Sensually Intelligent Massage in the previous chapter. Nothing we did had anything to do with her husband, because that's not how Sensual Intelligence works. She needed to feel herself as the divine, beautiful, mysterious gift that she was, and fill herself up with *that* reality, rather than the fetishized, exoticized, docile sex vixen her husband wanted her to be. As long as she was operating from a perceived deficit on her part, and as long as her husband's voice was the primary driver, there would be no real, lasting healing. She had to illuminate the treasure of herself.

Now, Gina is a successful entrepreneur. She is vibrant and sassy, and not at all the small, tamed woman she was when we first met. And, she left her husband and is in a relationship with a partner who truly adores her in her power.

This is the experience of life that is available to us from learning SQ. When we are able to see and experience each other in all of our nuance, depth, beauty, and sensual complexity, and let go of the fear of the body, a whole world becomes available.

I imagine a future in which Sensual IQ is practiced universally and allows us to access vitality and richness in life's expression and experience. A sense of connection and creativity. A way to be in joy and harmony with our own selves, and in clear communication with others.

SQ is the ability to be in your body with joy, to be fully in your expression, and to be able to connect with others in a way that is ever-evolving. It's joining the innocence and energy of childhood with the wisdom and discernment of adulthood and experience. I created this book, and teach as I do, to bring these things to life and have free conversations about what is really going on.

One of the biggest atrocities we have as a society is the loss of our close-knit communities, elders, community investment, and accountability. How many women get thrown under the bus when their community, church, school, etc, who was well aware of the abuse that was occurring, ignore the signs and turn their heads? I feel this can only happen because *everyone* is not practicing what I am proposing in this book. If you have a community of embodied, self-loving, mindful people, then there is true connection and compassion.

Change starts with the self and is played out in the community. As we inspire and influence one another with joyful respect for our bodies, then we can start making changes in our community. My proposal is that all communities practice SQ. We put SQ practices in the police force. Share this practice in the bible belt, with blue-collar workers who are busting their asses just to provide for their families, to the owners of the companies whose workers are working themselves to the bone.

This type of change will not happen just because one person has done this work. However, it will *never* happen if no one ever does this work. What I am proposing is a step in the direction of consent and sovereignty for everyone. It is only then that we can change the systems. But we cannot change the system without first changing the individuals who create and maintain those systems: *us*. We have to start somewhere, and my proposal is finding Sensual Intelligence.

It is time for spaces where bodies can feel beautiful, powerful, and full of joy. The aging body, the pregnant body, the body post-cancer, the body post-injury, the body after weight loss or gain; the body that is in the public eye, or has a new job, or is out in the elements—all of these changes to our bodies require the presence and consciousness of Sensual Intelligence.

It is so important to be in the practice of Sensual Intelligence as a way of life, not as a goal because our bodies are constantly shifting, and it takes practice to create awareness, acceptance, appreciation, attention, and artful application. Being deep in the practice of sensual intelligence will make it so that these inevitable shifts can be more easily integrated.

This is my invitation to you.

The journey of finding Sensual IQ involves an incredible amount of deep work, internal looking, forgiveness, loving, and listening in order to disconnect from a narrative of "should" and heal into a narrative of yourself. It is a journey of weaving love and forgiveness with the pain and shame, of honoring and dancing with your body that holds all of these stories. It is time to take ownership of your own life and what you want to create.

This is not just a journey for you to feel good, but it is the whole culture, the whole framework about how we do life, relationships, and work. This is all intricately connected to Sensual IQ.

This all starts with our own bodies. We teach our children through our actions and are role models of self-love. Finding the lost IQ is a revolutionary act that will pave the way for the next generation to experience respect, love, power, and leadership that honors the full spectrum of their intelligence: IQ, EQ, and SQ.

Sensual Intelligence is the space to be who we are: complex beings with a taste for the bitter, salty, sour, pungent, as well as the sweet. The richness of life is not solely about seeking pleasure. It is so much more than that. The whole of who we are and what we can become is found through sensing what *is*, and gaining pleasure from that truth. The truth ain't always sweet, but it's damned good.

ACKNOWLEDGEMENTS

This has been an amazing journey and I want to give love-filled gratitude to the people who really supported me and believed in me before even I did.

My Grandfather, Dr. Robert Lee Williams, for showing me that I can be an author. My dad and my pops for your love and support. Mike, the unwitting catalyst of this book journey. I wouldn't have started this without you. Marci, Deborah, Jill, and Randy for your faith and women in leadership. Nisha Moodley, incredible leader, friend, and inspiration. Lucia and Carolyn, you both held my heart and held it down during the long lonely months. Thank you for being my friends. Oliver, my first reader and editor. You worked a miracle on the initial manuscript. You're an angel. Colan, for your quiet yet ever present support and love. Thank you for believing in me. Shannon and Tom, thank you for your love, friendship, and helping Sensual Intelligence grow. Darby, Sarah, Leila, Grace, and Thandiwe, the women of my heart and my sanity. Moises for filling me with joy, love, and hope again. Val for being my writing partner and witnessing the process. And Oscar, the best kitty ever.

To everyone who is not named here, you are in my heart and I am so incredibly grateful for your love, support.

ABOUT THE AUTHOR

Shawnrey is the Sensual Intelligence™ and Embodiment Coach, teaching and inspiring people to embody their joy, pleasure, and self-love.

She blends 15+ years of dance and performance art, erotic poetry, sensual intimacy coaching, mindfulness, and nude live art modeling to connect mind, body, spirit, and pleasure.

She believes that we can change the world starting with our relationships with our own bodies.

You can find her on Instagram: @ShawnreyNotto, Facebook: ShawnreySQ, and her website: www.Shawnrey.com.

WORK WITH ME

If you would like help with finally feeling free in your heart and body so that you can come into your power, pleasure, and joy, you can find out more here: www.Shawnrey.com.

Whether or not you desire to join me for any future workshops or courses, I would love to hear about your Sensual Intelligence journey! Feel free to message me Shawnrey@Shawnrey.com and let me know how you are doing and how your life has changed as a result of embodying your full self-expression and sensual self-love.

You can also find me on Instagram: @ShawnreyNotto, Facebook: ShawnreySQ, and Twitter.

CAN YOU HELP?

Thank you for reading Sensual Intelligence: The Lost IQ!

It has been such a pleasure sharing all of this with you.

I would LOVE to hear what you have to say and greatly appreciate your feedback.

It takes a community to grow and improve. I need your input to make the next version of this book (and future books) better.

Please leave me an honest review on Amazon, letting me know what you thought.

Thanks so much!

www.ingramcontent.com/pod-product-compliance
Lightning Source LLC
Chambersburg PA
CBHW030904080526
44589CB00010B/134